D0391852

Charge It
on the
Master's Card

Charge It on the Master's Card

Charles Haddon Spurgeon
with a little help from
RANDY PETERSEN

 Fleming H. Revell
A Division of Baker Book House
Grand Rapids, Michigan 49516

© 1998 by Randy Petersen

Published by Fleming H. Revell
a division of Baker Book House Company
P.O. Box 6287, Grand Rapids, MI 49516-6287

Adapted from *Checque Book of the Bank of Faith* by Charles Haddon Spurgeon.

Printed in the United States of America

Library of Congress Cataloging-in-Publication Data

Spurgeon, C. H. (Charles Haddon), 1834–1892.
    Charge it on the Master's card / Charles Haddon Spurgeon ; edited by Randy Petersen.
    p. cm.
    Rev. ed. of: The cheque book of the Bank of Faith.
    ISBN 0-8007-5667-3
    1. Devotional calendars. I. Petersen, Randy. II. Spurgeon, C. H. (Charles Haddon), 1834–1892. Cheque book of the Bank of Faith. III. Title.
    BV4811.S66   1998
    242'.2—dc21   98-7410

Chapters 3, 11, and 42 are from Spurgeon's book *Evening by Evening*. Chapter 6 is from his book *Morning by Morning*.

For current information about all releases from Baker Book House, visit our web site:
                          http://www.bakerbooks.com

Contents

Preface

Charles Haddon Spurgeon was fifteen when he wandered into a tiny Methodist church during a blizzard. The church's regular preacher didn't show, and the fill-in was dreadful, mispronouncing words and repeating the same thought again and again. But as the sermon drew to a close, the substitute preacher saw Charles and asked if he wanted to accept Jesus as his Savior. Charles said yes, surprising even himself.

That began a lifelong love affair with Jesus Christ. If you get anything from the many commentaries and devotional books that Spurgeon wrote, it's this: The guy was absolutely bonkers about the Lord. And this: He wanted everyone else to feel the same way.

Spurgeon was only nineteen when he landed a job as pastor of New Park Street Church in London. He was a country bumpkin, to be sure, but there was something about him. He could get a crowd riled up like nobody's business. The previous pastor was dignified and respected, but the board wanted to shake things up a bit. That's exactly what young Spurgeon did.

Controversy followed Spurgeon like a puppy dog, and he must have been awfully fond of it. In his lengthy preaching and writing career, he dared to challenge Christians on all sides: the hyper Calvinists, the ultra-

Arminians, the stuffy Anglicans, his own Baptists. He told the truth as he saw it portrayed in the Bible, and if it offended people, so what?

But it was also the *way* he said things. The last half of the 1800s in London was a time of snobbery. Proper Englishmen spoke in lofty language, taking fifty words to say politely what a more direct speaker could say in five. Spurgeon went for the five. His speaking and writing were crammed with crisp words, sharp phrases, and colorful images. He was part journalist, part poet, as he unfolded the wonders of God.

Spurgeon died in 1892, at the age of fifty-eight. The original form of this book, *Checque Book of the Bank of Faith,* a collection of meditations on the promises of God, was written late in Spurgeon's life.

Cut to the present day.

Our task: to let Spurgeon speak to a new generation; to take selections from a daily devotional and essentially translate them for an audience of teenage Americans on the verge of the twenty-first century. *Translate* is an appropriate word. Spurgeon's English is different from ours. To give his words the power they had a dozen decades ago, we need to recast them.

- American English is different from British English. This occurs in certain words and spellings, but also in cadence. There's a rhythm that feels comfortable in British English but not in American, and vice versa. For the text to "sing," we need to adopt modern American rhythms.
- The language itself has changed in the last century. Though Spurgeon was clearly ahead of his time, his choice of words doesn't always fly in today's world.
- The world was different then. Spurgeon lived before cars cruised the streets or jets sliced the sky.

The telephone was brand-new. He knew no Internet. He refers regularly to the stuff of life, the technology of his world. We need to apply that to our world.

- Spurgeon lived in a Christian culture. American culture, like it or not, is becoming post-Christian— especially among the youngest generations. We cannot assume that kids know the Bible or anything about the Bible. Therefore, Spurgeon's many passing allusions to Scripture must be explained or adjusted.
- Teen culture is different from adult culture. Spurgeon could talk about work, marriage, or child-rearing, assuming that his readers (adults) would identify. We need to adjust those references to school, friendships, or parent-minding.

Given these factors, we treated this as a translation project. We've chosen a kind of "dynamic equivalence" method for most of it, and a freer paraphrase in other sections. The idea is, What would Spurgeon say to kids today?

He would certainly refer to the activities and technology of their world, though he probably wouldn't support their celebrity worship. He would certainly try to speak their language, but not to the point of trendy slang that sounds weird coming from adults anyway. He would understand that many kids don't have a knowledge of Scripture, and he'd try to explain the Bible stories he was referring to.

Sure, some purists will hate this whole thing, but the more we've worked on this, the more we feel that Charles H. would like what we've done. His whole ministry involved getting people psyched about the Lord, and he didn't care about sounding proper. In his day he gave a simple message to the common people. Well, now there's a generation an ocean and a century away that desperately needs to hear this message—and we feel that he'd do whatever it takes to get it to them.

So glory to God and thanks to one of his great servants, Charles Haddon Spurgeon. If we've overstepped any bounds, we're sure they both will forgive us.

Randy Petersen, 1998

1

Snakebite

I will put enmity between you and the woman, and between your offspring and hers; he will crush your head, and you will strike his heel (Genesis 3:15).

This is the first promise God made after Adam and Eve sinned. It sounds pretty violent, doesn't it? But if you look closely, you'll see the essence of God's whole plan for the human race.

Who is the offspring of the woman? Well, we're all the children of Eve in a way, but this is speaking of a specific person, the Lord Jesus.

And what's this head-crushing and heel-striking business? This is what happened when Jesus died on the cross. According to this verse, it was as if Jesus had stepped on a snake! He was wounded by the power of sin, and that "snakebite" hurt him a lot. But in the process he crushed the head of the snake, taking away the power of Satan. We're still waiting for the final fulfillment of this promise when Jesus returns, but the deathblow was dealt at Calvary.

What does this promise mean to us? Well, we too can be snakebitten by the power of evil, but we know we will triumph with Christ. So remember this as you go through this book. You will face temptation and maybe even give in to it. You will see evil all around you. You will feel the serpent's fangs in your heel, and you may even have to limp for a while. But remember the head-crushing! Jesus Christ, your Lord and friend, will tromp on that nasty snake.

2
Head-Crushing

The God of peace will soon crush Satan under your feet (Romans 16:20).

Remember the head-crushing!

Yesterday's verse gave us the promise that Jesus would crush the serpent, that he would win the victory over the powers of evil. But here's a new wrinkle: The old snake is going to be crushed under *our* feet.

The serpent will trip you up if you're not watching your step, but he will get the worst of it.

Who is doing this head-crushing? The God of peace. Remember, it's not *your* skill or power that triumphs over evil, but *God's*. So when you feel weak and battered by the forces of evil, trust the God of peace to give you some rest. You can "boldly go where no one has gone before"—because your God will clear the snakes out of the way.

Notice the simple word *soon*. This seems to have two meanings to it. First, we look forward to the Lord's coming and his final victory. But we also see God's work now, in our daily grind.

3

Superhighway in the Desert

A voice of one calling in the desert, "Prepare the way for the Lord, make straight paths for him. Every valley shall be filled in, every mountain and hill made low. The crooked roads shall become straight, the rough ways smooth" (Luke 3:4–5).

We need to respond to this call, paving a road for the Lord in our hearts and through the desert of our nature. Look at the four directions mentioned.

1. *"Every valley shall be filled in . . ."* We must give up our lowest thoughts—thoughts of doubt and despair as well as lust and selfish pleasure. Across these deep valleys, we must construct a multi-lane freeway of grace.

2. *"Every mountain and hill made low . . ."* Any proud feelings of self-sufficiency and boastful self-righteousness must be leveled to make a highway for the King of Kings. The Lord respects the lowly and humble but hates the haughty.

3. *"The crooked roads shall become straight . . ."* If your commitment is wavering, mark out a straight course for yourself, deciding to follow Christ in holiness. Be honest and true, knowing that God sees exactly what's in your heart.

4. *"The rough ways [shall become] smooth."* Remove the stumbling blocks of sin and pull out the thornbushes of rebellion. When the mighty Lord comes to visit you, you don't want him to have to pick his way through rubble.

Get God's highway ready in your heart and let him ride it!

Relax!

Bow and sword and battle I will abolish from the land,
so that all may lie down in safety (Hosea 2:18).

Imagine a world with no weapons. No terrorists. No civil wars. No riots. No nuclear arsenals. No germ warfare.

That's the picture God gives Hosea. He will give peace to his people.

Promises like this usually have two angles. There will be utter peace in God's future kingdom, but we can also expect a personal peace in our lives.

The beginning of this verse speaks of peace "with the beasts of the field and the birds of the air and the creatures that move along the ground." We might think of these as earthly enemies, supernatural evils, and other little annoyances. Any of these could keep us from lying down comfortably, but they won't. The Lord will remove these threats.

So we can relax! Quit fretting about every little thing. God offers you safety. When you belong to the God of peace, it is safer to lie down and relax than to sit up and worry.

Remember that gem from the Twenty-third Psalm? "He makes me lie down in green pastures" (verse 2). Stop thinking of your Christian life as a constant battle and let the Comforter comfort you.

5

Oops!

I will strengthen you and help you (Isaiah 41:10).

Have you ever been in a tough situation, when you reached down deep for that extra strength you needed—and it wasn't there?

Maybe you were in a heated conversation, and instead of saying something wise and brilliant, you burst into tears.

Maybe you were working on a difficult project, and just when you knew you had to stick with it and get it done, you gave up.

Maybe you were facing temptation, and suddenly realizing the right thing to do, you decided to do the wrong thing.

Here's some good news for you: God has all the strength you need. In today's verse he promises to let us use it. When we are feeling weak and wounded, he will feed our souls and heal our hearts. There is no telling what God can do when we let his power work through us. You never need to come up empty again.

Hasn't this ever happened to you?

In that family argument, God gave you the humility you needed.

In that time of panic, God helped you stay calm.

When your heart was broken, God whispered his love to you.

The fact is, God gives unexpected strength when we face unexpected trials. We may think of ourselves as weak and cowardly, but God's strength can make us superheroes.

6

Big Shoulders

Cast all your anxiety on him because he cares for you (1 Peter 5:7).

Why do you look so worried all the time? It makes people think that you don't really believe this promise: The Lord cares for you. The weight that's making you stagger wouldn't even faze your heavenly Father. Your crushing burden would be his speck of dust.

So be patient. God has not forgotten you. The one who feeds sparrows will also give you what you need. Don't let despair drag you down. There is always hope. Menacing storm clouds yield refreshing showers, and the darkest night gives way to dawn. God loves you just as much in tough times as in happy times. He will bandage your wounds and heal your broken heart.

What would your life be like if you would just let the caring Lord care for you? In a terrible famine Elijah had just a day's worth of food, but he trusted God to provide—and the food lasted many days (1 Kings 17). God will provide for you too. If you trust him with your soul, why not trust him with your body as well? Throw your anxiety onto his mighty shoulders!

Under the Fig Tree

Jesus said, "You believe because I told you I saw you under the fig tree. You shall see greater things than that" (John 1:50).

We're not sure what was going on under the fig tree, but we do know Nathanael was ready to believe in Jesus just because of this one thing. That may seem strange to those who take time to question and ponder. But the fact is, Nathanael was ready to believe. Like a child, he was willing to open his eyes to what Jesus would show him.

But too often we shut our eyes and are blind to the wonderful things God is doing.

As a Christian, you have "seen" some great things already. Jesus has come into your life and changed some things. But don't stop there! Open your eyes and see what more he can do!

There are greater truths in God's Word.

Greater depths of experience.

Greater heights of fellowship.

Greater ways he can use us.

Greater discoveries of power, love, and wisdom.

If we are willing to trust God, he will show us all this. So let's keep our eyes on spiritual things and expect to see more and more.

Don't think of your life as the same old grind, grinding down to nothing. See yourself growing, growing in God's grace and greatness, until we finally see him in all his glory.

8

Seeing God

Blessed are the pure in heart, for they will see God (Matthew 5:8).

There is a strong connection between what we love and what we see. If we love to do what's wrong, it's hard to see what's right. If our hearts are dirty, our eyes won't focus very well. That's what Jesus is saying here. How can you see the glory of a holy God when you love to do unholy things?

So shoot for purity—purity of heart. Let the Spirit clean you up on the inside, and let your outside behavior be marked by obedience to God's Word.

And what a great experience it is to see God! How does that happen? In Jesus. When you're pure in heart, you can look at Jesus, as described in Scripture, and see God's truth, God's love, God's plans and promises—all wrapped up in this one person, Jesus Christ.

With clean hearts we look forward to the day when Jesus will return. The apostle John wrote, "We know that when he appears, we shall be like him, for *we shall see him as he is*" (1 John 3:2). Our hope in his coming makes us want to keep ourselves clean. We want to see him clearly, without worrying about any bad stuff fouling up our hearts and dimming our vision. "Everyone who has this hope in him," John continued, "purifies himself, just as he is pure" (verse 3).

What you love affects how you see. Keep loving Jesus with all your heart.

Giving and Gaining

A generous man will prosper (Proverbs 11:25).

If you want to be a true success, you must not cling selfishly to the money you make—you need to give it freely to the poor. Being stingy may be the world's path to prosperity, but it is not God's way. We read in the previous verse, "One man gives freely, but gains even more; another withholds unduly, but comes to poverty" (Proverbs 11:24).

Faith's way of gaining is giving.

Time after time it works this way. If you give freely to those in need, God will graciously reward you with a certain amount of prosperity—whatever amount is good for you.

Of course, this doesn't mean you'll get rich. Getting rich is like getting fat. It may be fun to eat all sorts of rich foods, but they may give you indigestion and eventually heart trouble, not to mention the extra pounds you'll have to carry around. No, you want to be just fat enough to be healthy, and just rich enough to be content.

But there is a mental and spiritual richness that I long to have. And the principle of today's verse applies here too. As long as I have generous thoughts toward God, toward the church, and toward other people, God will make me spiritually wealthy. But if I'm a tightwad with my thoughts, my heart will starve.

Let's be generous and giving—just like our Lord. After all, he gave himself for us. Can we begrudge him anything in return?

10

The Secret Spring

He who refreshes others will himself be refreshed (Proverbs 11:25).

There's a promise here that applies in many parts of life: The way I treat others affects the way God treats me.

If I care for others, meeting their needs, God will see that my needs are met. If I remember the poor, God will remember me. If I look after little children, the Lord will treat me as his child. If I "feed God's flock," giving them instruction in God's truth, God will feed me too. If I "water his garden," helping young Christians grow, God will turn my soul into a well-watered garden.

On the other hand, I may focus on myself, morbidly obsessing about my own needs. I may analyze my own feelings until I don't feel anything anymore. I may complain about my own weaknesses until I'm too weak to complain.

But it makes a lot more sense to be unselfish, to care for the people around me. I do this simply out of love for my Lord Jesus, but it's profitable for me too.

So if your reservoir is running low and there's no rain in the forecast to replenish it, what do you do? Let the water out. Let it refresh all the withering plants around you. If you let that happen, you'll see something amazing: Your reservoir will fill up even as the water flows out.

You see, there's a secret source, a spring that flows into your reservoir—but when you close up your resources, you plug up the spring. Your hoarded water gets stagnant and the fresh springwater can't get in. But once you let your love flow out to others, the Lord's love will flow into your heart with revitalizing power. Praise God!

11

He Prays for Us

Simon, Simon, Satan has asked to sift you as wheat. But
I have prayed for you, Simon, that your faith may not
fail (Luke 22:31–32).

Think about it: Jesus prays for us. When we pray, he
pleads our case before the Father. And when we're not
praying, his prayers protect us from dangers we don't
even know about.

Note what he says to Simon Peter. "Satan has asked
to sift you as wheat. But . . ." But what?

"But go and pray for yourself"? That would be good
advice, but that's not what he said.

"But I will make you spiritually strong enough to defeat Satan"? That would be a great blessing, but that's
not what's written here.

"But I have prayed for you." That's it.

We have no idea how much we owe to our Savior's
prayers. When we reach the heights of heaven and look
back at the big picture of our lives, we'll be mighty im-
pressed with the way Jesus undid the mischief Satan
was doing on earth.

And notice that our verse doesn't say, "Satan has been
sifting you," but that he had *asked*. Even before Satan
begins to tempt, Jesus nips it in the bud. He is there before the Father, pointing to the nail prints in his hands,
pleading our case, making sure that the temptation is
never greater than we can bear. Mercy outruns malice.

Nor does Jesus say, "I *want* to pray for you." He's already been doing it! He anticipates the ambush and pre-
pares us for it—even when we don't have a clue.

This is a reason to sing for joy, to thank the Lord, and
to live with new confidence.

12

Recycling

For the Lord will not cast off forever (Lamentations 3:31 KJV).

A girl may stop wearing her favorite earrings or bracelets for a few days, but she won't forget about them entirely—and she won't throw them in the trash. In the same way, the Lord does not discard the people he loves—though sometimes it may seem that way for a short time.

Some Christians talk about being "in grace" or "out of God's will," as if we were rabbits running in and out of our burrows. But it's not that way at all. The Lord's love is a more permanent matter than that.

From the beginning of time, and even before that, he chose us to be part of his family. And he will love us till the end of time, and beyond that. He loved us so much that he died for us, so we can be sure his love will never die.

In fact, God has staked his reputation on his love for us. He can't stop loving us any more than he can stop being King of Glory! He is a faithful husband who will never divorce his beloved bride.

So do you feel as if God has thrown you in the trash? Toss that thought in the trash instead. The Lord does not discard his people; he will love you forever.

13

No Slamming

Whoever comes to me I will never drive away (John 6:37).

Has there ever been a case in which someone came to Jesus and was turned away? Nope. And there never will be.

Even among the souls in hell, not one of them can say, "I went to Jesus and he didn't want to see me." So do you think you're the exception to this rule? Forget it. He will not turn you away!

What do you want to talk to Jesus about? Are you bothered by stuff that's going on at your job, in your school, in your family, in your world? Then tell him about it. I'm telling you, he *will* grant you an audience. Whether you go to him every day or whether this will be your first time, let's go together and share our thoughts with the Lord. You'll see: He won't slam the door of grace in your face.

Do you know what Jesus' enemies said about him? "This man welcomes sinners and eats with them" (Luke 15:2). That's good news for sinners like you and me. We come to him in weakness and sin, with trembling faith, little knowledge, and slender hope, but he does not reject us. We come to him through prayer, but broken prayer; with confession, but faulty confession; with praise, but praise that's far short of what he deserves. But still he loves to listen to us.

Let him hear from you today.

14

The Rest Is . . . Wonderful

> Come to me, all you who are weary and burdened, and
> I will give you rest (Matthew 11:28).

What a great gift! Jesus gives us rest. We cannot buy it or borrow it; we must accept it as a gift.

You may be slaving away, toiling under the whip of ambition, greed, lust, or anxiety—but he will set you free from your slavery and give you rest.

You may be burdened, weighed down with sin, fear, worry, or sorrow—but he will lift that load off your back if you come to him. Remember, he carried the crushing weight of our sin so we don't have to carry it.

Jesus gives rest. Do you believe it? Will you try it out? Come to Jesus and stop looking for rest everywhere else. His gift of rest is deep, safe, holy, and eternal. Of course, it will be finalized in heaven, but he will start giving it to you today.

15

Poor but Precious

The needy will not always be forgotten (Psalm 9:18).

It's tough when you're poor, but if you trust in the Lord, you're rich. It may feel as if you were absent the day God handed out wealth and prosperity, but know this: God has not forgotten you. Someday this will all be set right. If you feel like Lazarus, the poor man in Jesus' parable, you won't always be begging at the rich man's gate. Someday you'll rest in heavenly bliss.

But we don't just wait for someday. We know that even now the Lord is remembering his poor but precious children. "Yet I am poor and needy," said the psalmist; "may the Lord think of me. You are my help and my deliverer; O my God, do not delay" (Psalm 40:17).

In fact, poor people who trust in the Lord can expect great things. They expect the Lord to provide them with everything they need to live and serve him; they expect all things to work together for their good; they expect to know Jesus better, even in their poverty (remember that he had nowhere to lay his head); and they expect to share his glory when he comes again.

The poor believer has many songs to sing that the rich sinner cannot understand. So even when there's not much food on your plate here below, think of the feast that's waiting for you above.

16

Who's Calling?

Everyone who calls on the name of the LORD will be saved (Joel 2:32).

So why don't you call on his name? Why do you run to this friend or that one with all your worries, when God is right there, ready to hear your faintest call? Why do you sit down and devise elaborate schemes, inventing plans to get you out of your troubles? Why don't you just dump your problems on the Lord?

Any sprinter will tell you that the fastest way to run is straight ahead—so why don't you go straight to God? If you look for satisfaction anywhere else, you'll come up empty. But you're sure to find it with God. He backs it up with his promise.

Oh, but maybe you're wondering if God's promise really applies to you. Read the verse again. See that word *everyone?* That means you. It means anyone who calls out to God.

Maybe you're desperate; you don't know where to turn. Maybe you don't know how even God will be able to turn your life around. But that's not your business. He made the promise; he'll find a way to keep it. You're not in charge here; let the Lord call the shots. Just call on him, and he will save you.

Facing Pharaoh

God said, "I will be with you" (Exodus 3:12).

God was sending Moses on an errand. Nothing major. Just going to the mightiest king on earth and demanding freedom for his people.

This was ridiculous! How could a wise God send one lonely Israelite up against Pharaoh and all the forces of Egypt? This would be a huge risk, requiring enormous power, far beyond the abilities of Moses.

Except for one thing: God would be there too.

The same thing can work in your life. When God asks you to do something, he will go with you. If you rely on his power and work for his glory (not your own), you can trust that he will be right by your side.

What more could you ask? You could have all the angels and archangels with you, and you still might fail. But if God is with you, success is guaranteed.

So don't do your errands for God in a timid way or halfheartedly or carelessly. If God is with you, how should you act? Boldly, confidently. You can face the Pharaohs of this world without fear.

18

Love Story

Though the LORD makes his life a guilt offering, he will see his offspring and prolong his days (Isaiah 53:10).

Jesus did not die in vain. His death was sacrificial: He died as our substitute, because death was the penalty for our sins. God accepted this substitution, so we are saved from eternal death. By dying, Jesus became like a seed planted in the ground—though the seed itself dies, it brings forth a new plant that bears a lot of fruit. In the same way, Jesus' death has created a new family—"offspring" in a way, people who have been saved by Jesus' death.

Sometimes when you look at a friend, you can see a strong resemblance to his or her parents. Likewise, you should be able to see Christ in Christians.

Often a child will take up the career of a mother or father, in a way extending the parent's work into the next generation. In the same way, Jesus' life is prolonged through his children, all the believers.

Jesus is alive and he is seeing his offspring. He watches us as we go through our lives, and he delights in us. The eyes that once wept for us are now viewing us with pleasure. He looks at those who are looking toward him. Our eyes meet. (What a great love story!)

19

Saved

If you confess with your mouth, "Jesus is Lord," and believe in your heart that God raised him from the dead, you will be saved (Romans 10:9).

Have you confessed with your mouth? Have you openly told people what you believe about Jesus, that he's your Lord and Savior, that God raised him from the dead?

Do you believe this in your heart? Do you trust in Jesus as your only hope of salvation?

If, in all honesty before God, you can answer yes to both questions—you are saved! That's what today's text says. It doesn't say you *might* be saved, but that you *are*. It's as plain as the nose on your face, as clear as a cloudless sky—"You will be saved."

As a believer and a confessor, you can grab that promise and bring it before God—today, tomorrow, the day you die, or on judgment day.

What do you need to be saved from? From sin, from the power sin holds over you, from the punishment that comes as a result of sin, and ultimately from the very existence of sin. God has said it—"You will be saved." You can believe it. Glory be to God!

20

Overcoming

> To him who overcomes, I will give the right to eat from the tree of life, which is in the paradise of God (Revelation 2:7).

What does it mean to overcome? It's the language of warfare—we must win the battle. What battle? Well, for one thing, we are to overcome the false prophets in the world and the evil teaching they spread. What is the false teaching you have to deal with each day? Whatever it is, hold the line. Be courageous for the truth.

Many of us also need to overcome our own fear. What will people think of us when we stand up for the truth? You might also have to overcome your tendency to drift away from your devotion to Christ. It's easy sometimes to go with the flow, and hard to keep Christ at the center of your life.

But if we do overcome, today's verse gives us a great picture. We're admitted to the very center of God's paradise, past the guard-angel with the fiery sword, right up to the tree of life. So we'll escape the endless death that results from sin, and we'll gain an everlasting life with God in innocence and holiness.

So when you find yourself embattled, don't lose heart! If you fight well and overcome, you'll walk with God in paradise.

21

Walk like an Egyptian

The Egyptians will know that I am the LORD (Exodus 7:5).

Sometimes it's hard to talk about the Lord with those who don't know him. We begin to feel like Israelites enslaved in Egypt. The "Egyptians" around us worship various idols or act as if there were no God at all.

But don't be discouraged when these people don't listen to you. God has a way of getting his point across. He can break proud hearts and bring skeptics to their knees.

In Egypt he used ten plagues to set his people free. This was a powerful way of letting the Egyptians know who he is—the true and living God. None of the Israelites died in these plagues, and none of them drowned in the Red Sea. God saved them, as he saves us. Then and now God reveals his Godship by delivering his people. And in the future when we are glorified—invited to live and reign with God in heaven—even the most obstinate of God's enemies will finally acknowledge that this is the true God.

I pray that the Holy Spirit would shake this world with the convincing power of God's truth until everyone bows before Jesus and calls him Lord.

22

Regarding the Weak

> Blessed is he who has regard for the weak; the LORD delivers him in times of trouble (Psalm 41:1).

It is our Christian duty to think about the poor and needy. Jesus assured us that whatever we do for "the least of these brothers of mine"—and he was talking about hungry people, sick people, poor people—we are doing those same things for him (Matthew 25:40).

Many people just sort of throw money at the poor without thinking about it. Others give nothing at all. But today's verse gives a promise to those who *regard* the weak—looking into their situation, figuring out ways to help them, and following through on those ideas. We can do more with care than with cash—and even more with both of those put together.

If we regard the weak, we will be regarded by God in our own times of weakness. If we pay attention to the needs of those around us, God will pay special attention to our needs.

This psalm doesn't promise that we will avoid trouble. No matter how generous we are to others, we will encounter some needy times ourselves. But in those times, we can put in a special claim for the Lord's help, and he will be true to his word.

You may have heard the phrase "God helps those who help themselves." That's often quoted by rich misers who trust only in their own resources. But today's verse says something very different: God helps those who help *others*.

As you have done to others, so will God do to you. Empty your pockets.

23

Claim It!

He is to lay his hand on the head of the burnt offering,
and it will be accepted on his behalf to make atonement
for him (Leviticus 1:4).

In Old Testament times a worshiper brought an animal
to the altar, where it was sacrificed to pay for the person's sins. By this act of laying a hand on the animal's
head, the person "claimed" the sacrifice.

The same sort of thing happens with us, except Jesus
is our sacrificial offering, and we place on him the hand
of faith. If a bull or goat could be accepted in payment
for sin, how much more acceptable is the sinless life of
Jesus?

This whole idea of sacrifice and substitution may
seem strange to you, but it is at the heart of our faith. It
is our hope, our joy, the only thing we have to boast
about. By ourselves we are unacceptable—but Jesus is
accepted and we're with him.

Have you ever laid your hand on Jesus' sacrifice? I
mean, have you ever claimed his death as the payment
for *your* sins? If you haven't, do it now. Jesus is yours
now if you will have him.

Lean on him. Lean hard on him—he can hold you.
By his blood you are brought into God's family, your sins
are wiped clean, and you are the Lord's.

Foot Fall

He will guard the feet of his saints (1 Samuel 2:9).

The road is slippery and our feet are worn out, but the Lord will guard our feet. If we entrust ourselves to him in obedient faith, he will take care of us. In another verse he promises to send guardian angels to watch over us, but here he says he himself will be our guardian.

If you're walking down the street and you fall, what happens? Your clothes get dirty or torn, you get nasty scrapes on your knees or hands, and you can bet that someone has seen you and is laughing like crazy. The same dangers exist in a spiritual sense. We can easily fall into the false ideas of the people around us or take on some of their sinful ways.

But God guards our feet better than any hundred-dollar sneakers can! He keeps our feet from swelling and blistering or growing too weary as we try to follow his ways. He keeps our feet from getting cut on sharp rocks or bitten by poisonous snakes, and he protects our souls from being wounded by the evil around us. He keeps us from getting our feet caught and stumbling, and he warns us away from the traps of those who want to hurt us.

With this promise we can walk—and live—with no weariness and no fear.

25

Get Real

He comes to men and says, "I sinned, and perverted what was right, but I did not get what I deserved. He redeemed my soul from going down to the pit, and I will live to enjoy the light" (Job 33:27–28).

When someone comes with a sincere confession of sin, the Lord welcomes that person with open arms. In fact, he's always on the lookout for those who are in trouble because of what they've done wrong.

And can't we all echo these words? Haven't we all sinned? Haven't we all sinned *willfully*, perverting what is right? And haven't we all discovered that crime doesn't pay?

All God asks is that we come to him with this honest acknowledgment. We can do no less.

We can plead for forgiveness in the name of Jesus. The pit of hell may yawn before us, but Jesus rescues us, granting us life and light. There is no need for despair or even doubt. The Lord does not mock humble souls—he means what he says. The guilty can be forgiven. Those who deserve the death penalty can receive a free pardon.

Lord, we confess our sins, and we ask you to forgive!

26

Defying the Devil

There is no sorcery against Jacob, no divination against Israel (Numbers 23:23).

This should smash to bits any of your silly, superstitious fears. Even if there's any truth in witchcraft and the occult, they cannot affect the people of the Lord. Devils cannot curse those whom God blesses.

This verse concerns Balaam, the false prophet who cunningly plotted to overthrow Israel. And there will always be ungodly people who attempt that sort of thing. But even with all their secret plans, they are doomed to fail. Their weapons misfire. Their light-sabres fizzle out.

Let them weave their webs—we will not be caught in them. Even if they call on the prince of darkness, employing his snakelike craft, it won't do them any good. Their spells will not work.

What a comfort this is for us! We may, like Jacob, wrestle with God, but no one else will be able to wrestle us and win. We don't need to be afraid—either of Satan himself or of any secret enemies with deep, deceitful conspiracies. They cannot hurt those who trust in the living God. We defy the devil and all his armies.

27

Precious Stones

There you will remember your conduct and all the actions by which you have defiled yourselves, and you will loathe yourselves for all the evil you have done (Ezekiel 20:43).

Where does this happen? In God's presence, when we stand in his grace, peace, and safety. That's where we will be led to repent of all the ways we have mistreated our gracious God.

Repentance is a precious diamond. God gives it to us as one of the perks of salvation. That's right. He not only receives our repentance but also *gives* us the ability and desire to repent. His promise of blood-bought pardon and undeserved mercy is enough to dissolve a heart of stone.

Do you feel your heart hardening? Focus your attention on God's loving forgiveness, and that should help you leave sin, lament sin, and loathe sin.

Ask God to give you this gift of penitence, helping you remember, repent, regret, and return to him.

Your tears of repentance would be a welcome watering of your heart's dry soil.

Lord, strike the rock of my heart, or speak to it, and cause the waters to flow!

28

No More Tears

He will wipe every tear from their eyes (Revelation 21:4).

If you're a believer, this is what you have to look forward to—an end to sorrow, all tears wiped away.

We live in a world of weeping, but it will pass away. Verse 1 of this chapter tells us there will be a new heaven and a new earth, so we won't have to cry over the way sin messed up the old earth. Verse 2 speaks of the wedding feast of the Lamb. This is a time for extreme happiness—tears would be out of place. Verse 3 says that God himself will live among us. The psalmist said that in his presence are "eternal pleasures" (Psalm 16:11). No time for tears.

What will it be like with no more sorrow, no tears, no pain? More glorious than you can imagine. If your eyes are red from weeping, look to the Lord, who will wipe away those tears. "Weeping may remain for a night," the Bible says, "but rejoicing comes in the morning" (Psalm 30:5).

Hurry, Lord, and turn our mourning to morning!

29

Bless You

> Be careful to obey all these regulations I am giving you, so that it may always go well with you and your children after you, because you will be doing what is good and right in the eyes of the LORD your God (Deuteronomy 12:28).

We are not saved by obeying God's law, but God still blesses us when we do. Deuteronomy pronounces blessings on those who do what God wants and curses on those who don't. Fortunately for us, Jesus took our curses upon himself, but the blessings remain in effect.

So we need to pay attention to what God has told us, not picking and choosing the parts we like but respecting "all these regulations." This is the path of blessing for parents and children alike, generation after generation. If families faithfully follow the Lord, he will bless them clearly and publicly.

If we practice dishonesty or double-dealing, we are straying from the path of blessing. Conforming to the world's unholy ways cannot bring us the good things we want. But things will go well with us when we go well with God. That which brings pleasure to God will also bring pleasure to us.

30

On the Go

> I am with you and will watch over you wherever you go (Genesis 28:15).

Two promises here: God's presence and his preservation. We need both of them, and we'll have them—as long as we're going places he wants us to go. If God leads us to move to another area, why should we be sad about that? Wherever we go, we are both pilgrims and strangers: The Lord is our true home, and he continues to be with us.

If we travel to foreign countries, even places of unrest, we are in no real danger. "I will watch over you," God says. What better passport could you want?

This promise was made to Jacob, a mama's boy, not an adventurer like his brother. Jacob was a homebody, but he was taking a trip, and God was going with him. He had little luggage and no traveling companions, and yet no prince ever had a better bodyguard. Even as he slept in the open field, angels watched over him, and the Lord spoke to him.

So if the Lord is telling you to go somewhere, your best response is, "Let's go!"

31

Hear! Hear!

My God will hear me (Micah 7:7).

Friends may betray us, but the Lord will not turn away. He keeps listening. A few verses earlier Micah warns, "Do not trust a neighbor; put no confidence in a friend" (Micah 7:5). That's an awful way to live, though sometimes it's necessary. Yet even in that sad state of affairs, our Best Friend remains true to us, and we can tell him how we feel.

So don't quarrel with your friends; it's wiser to look to the Lord for friendship. If your own relatives aren't paying enough attention to you, turn to the Lord. He promises to hear us, especially when others are treating us unkindly.

Because God is a living God, he can hear us.

Because God is a loving God, he will hear us.

Because God is a loyal God, he has to hear us.

If he is your God, you can say with confidence, "My God will hear me." So go ahead! Pour out your hurting heart to the Lord your God. He is listening.

32

Sunrise

For you who revere my name, the sun of righteousness
will rise with healing in its wings (Malachi 4:2).

This prophecy came true once in the coming of Jesus,
and it will come true again in his second coming. But it
also applies to our daily lives.

Does your life seem dark and murky, as if you're wandering around in the middle of a moonless night? Don't
worry, the sun will rise. When the night is darkest, the
dawn is nearest.

And this is no ordinary sun rising. It's *the* sun, the Sun
of Righteousness, every ray a beam of holiness. This
healer comes with justice as well as mercy. Jesus saves
us not only by his love but also by his holiness. Our salvation is not a matter of God bending the rules for us;
it's Jesus playing by the rules and paying our penalty.

The question is, Do you revere his name? Do you
honor God with worship and obedience? Then your
nighttime will be short, and the morning will bring an
end to your sickness and sorrow. Light, warmth, joy,
clear vision—the Sun will bring all this.

Has Jesus risen for you? Then bask in his sunshine.
Does it seem that he's hiding from you? Then wait for
his rising. Jesus will shine on you, as surely as the sun
will rise tomorrow.

33

Might as Well Jump

And you will go out and leap like calves released from the stall (Malachi 4:2).

Yesterday we talked about the Sun of Righteousness (Jesus) rising and bringing us healing. What happens when this Sun shines?

The bedridden get rid of their beds, walking outside to breathe the fresh air. Just as cattle take advantage of the sunny days of spring and summer to go out of the barn and romp on the hills, in the same way we can leave the stalls of our depression and frolic in the fields of holy confidence.

Why should you coop yourself up in your room? Get up, get out, live a little! Jesus said that his sheep would "come in and go out, and find pasture" (John 10:9). So get out there and start grazing in the rich meadows of God's love!

Those calves, born in the barn, will never build their leg muscles unless they go out to the field and leap around. Likewise, you won't grow as a Christian unless you leap a bit. So jump for joy! Try some new and different ways to worship God and share his love with others. The Sun of Righteousness has risen and is shining on you! Be like a flower, unfolding your heart's petals to the new day. Open up to him, expand, and grow.

34

Free Jewelry!

> He who did not spare his own Son, but gave him up for us all—how will he not also, along with him, graciously give us all things? (Romans 8:32).

This is more than a promise—it's a bundle of promises. Imagine a piece of jewelry with rubies, emeralds, and diamonds around a nugget of gold. That's what we have here.

There is no downside to this verse. We can't lose. After giving us Jesus, would God hold anything back from us? Whatever we need, in earth or heaven, he will give us. If he had any limit to his love, he certainly would have held back his own Son.

What do you need? Just ask for it. And you don't have to beg and plead, using pressure or extortion. God gives *freely.* After all, he freely gave his own Son—and come to think of it, who would have dared to ask him for that gift? It was his own idea, because that's what we needed.

So can't you trust God to be on top of your needs? If we had to use force to sway the all-powerful God, we'd have no chance. But his love rises on its own, like a mountain spring, and overflows to meet our needs.

35

I'll Be Back

I will not leave you as orphans; I will come to you (John 14:18).

Jesus was leaving his disciples to go back to heaven, but he wouldn't be gone forever. They could find comfort in the fact that he promised to come back. And today we have that same reality to look forward to. Jesus is already on his way here.

"I am coming soon!" he says in the last chapter of the Bible (Revelation 22:7). And here in John 14 he assures all his disciples, "I *will* come to you." No one can keep him from us or even delay him for half an hour. When he says it, he means it. "I will come *to you*," he says. He is coming to us and for us.

Yes, right now we're living in between his arrivals, and there are times when Jesus seems to hide himself from us. But he'll be back, in his full glory. He leaves us in a sense, but only in a sense. He leaves us with the phenomenal promise of his return.

Lord, come quickly! Life without you is hardly life at all. We long to see your sweet smile again. When are you coming? Hurry!

36

In Bold Blood

When I see the blood, I will pass over you (Exodus 12:13).

Can you stand the sight of blood? God can. In fact, he needs to see blood in order to save us.

This story from Exodus is a picture of what Christ did for us. God sent a deadly plague, but when he saw the blood on the Israelites' doorposts, he passed over those houses. In the same way, when he sees Jesus' blood, offered for us, he does not punish us as we deserve.

So when we consider the blood of Jesus, that "sight of blood" should actually be comforting to us. But even when our faith is fragile and we begin to question things, God's vision is still twenty-twenty. He sees the blood and spares us.

God knows the full meaning of Jesus' death. He is satisfied with the payment that has been made on our behalf. We know that after six days of creation, he looked at what he had made and said, "Excellent!" What must he be saying after witnessing the obedient sacrifice of his beloved Son? If he was well-pleased at the beginning of Jesus' ministry (Matthew 3:17), imagine how delighted he must have been at the end.

The Bible says that we are sprinkled with Christ's blood (Hebrews 10:22). That may seem a bit gory to you at first, but it's really a beautiful picture of our salvation. God sees Christ's blood on our hearts, and we are safe forever.

37

City Spin

All these blessings will come upon you and accompany
you if you obey the LORD your God: You will be blessed
in the city and blessed in the country (Deuteronomy
28:2–3).

The city is crammed with noise, activity, chaos, and pain,
with many temptations, pitfalls, fears. Many people
worry about living in the city or even visiting there. But
God's blessing takes the edge off that worry. He gives us
strength to meet the demands of the city and pleasure
in what we have to do there.

God's blessing may not make us great, but it will keep
us good. Honestly, it may not make us rich, but it will
keep us richly honest. Whether we are cashiers or cus-
todians, managers or merchants, God can make us truly
productive in the city.

Where's the best place to go fishing? Where the fish
are.

What if you're sharing God with people? You go where
the people are. You may prefer the peace and quiet of
country life, but if God wants you in the city, go. There's
plenty of work to do there.

So listen for the Lord to lead you, and be ready to
obey. We learn from today's verse: Obedience brings
blessing.

38

Makeover

If you return to the Almighty, you will be restored (Job 22:23).

Job's friend Eliphaz made this great comment, which sort of sums up the message of the whole Bible.

Is sin pulling you down, messing up your life? Have things in your life gone sour because of your pride or selfishness? If so, here's the first thing you need to do: return to the Lord.

Are you sorry for your sin? Do you trust Christ to make you clean again? Then say that to God.

When you think about it, it's the only plan that makes sense. As a Christian, you belong to God—so you can't find true happiness apart from him. And it's not too smart to keep fighting against the almighty Lord. He'll win. If you think things are bad now, just wait till he starts to discipline you.

But look at the bright side of this promise. Return to him and you'll be *restored*. You'll be like an old, dilapidated house that suddenly gets a makeover. Only God has the tools for that job, and he's waiting to start work. So don't delay. Confess your sins and get restored.

39

Right-Hand God

I will uphold you with my righteous right hand (Isaiah 41:10).

Are you ever afraid of falling? Stroll down an icy street or hike along a rocky mountain trail—does the prospect of falling flat on your face appeal to you? Of course not! It's natural to want something to hold on to, some railing, some guide, some strong arm of support.

That's what today's verse is talking about: God holds us up with his righteous right hand. In the Bible the right hand is the hand of strength and skill. Sorry, lefties.

And it's not only God's strength that holds us up but his righteousness as well. We are protected physically *and spiritually*. We may face some pretty terrifying dangers, but we can relax in God's "security force." If God is holding you up, demons can't pull you down.

Your feet may be weak, but God's right hand is strong. The road may be rough, but we can move ahead boldly, empowered by our almighty Lord. We will not fall if we lean on the one who holds up the whole universe.

40

You're Gold

> I will bring [my people] into the fire; I will refine them like silver and test them like gold. They will call on my name and I will answer them; I will say, "They are my people," and they will say, "The LORD is our God" (Zechariah 13:9).

God's grace turns us into precious metal. You've heard the phrase "Go for the gold!" You *are* the gold. And what happens to gold? It gets burned.

Seriously, gold and other precious metals were refined in a superheated furnace, where any impurities would be burned away. God is saying that his people will get the same treatment.

Are you still jazzed about being gold? Wouldn't it be better to be something else, something that didn't have to go into the furnace? Like a rock, maybe. There you go! A rock just sits in the field all day, minding its own business, no refining necessary.

Well, a rock's life is certainly easier, but it's not better. The Bible is full of stories of folks who chose rocks over gold—like Esau, who traded God's promises for a bowl of stew. Don't do that. Go for the gold. Be gold!

The fire only improves us, you see; it doesn't destroy us. We are brought through the fire, not left in it. Because the Lord values us so highly, he wants to purify us. We should welcome the refining process, happy to have our flaws melted away.

Lord, sometimes we feel that we are melting, that your refining fire is too hot. But this is the way you want to do things, and your way is best. Stay with us as you purify us, and complete the process.

Eyewitness News

You will be his witness to all men of what you have seen and heard (Acts 22:15).

Paul was knocked off his horse and blinded by a light from heaven. Just God's little way of getting his attention. After Jesus spoke to him, Paul was taken in by a prophet, who restored his sight and uttered this prophecy. Paul had been chosen to be a witness, and as we now know, his testimony would have a huge impact on the whole world.

But we fit into this verse too. We can tell others what the Lord has shown us.

Step 1: See and hear. It seems so obvious, but if we don't experience the Lord for ourselves, we'll have nothing to tell.

Step 2: Talk about it. Be eager to give your "eyewitness news" to others.

Remember that you are *his* witness. Jesus is the focus of your report and the power behind you. Let the truth and power of Jesus absorb you like a sponge.

And don't limit your witness to a few selected friends. You can share your story with "all men"—people everywhere, old, young, rich, poor, good, bad. Don't hold back.

Lord, help me give an honest testimony of how you have changed my life.

First Love

You have forsaken your first love (Revelation 2:4).

Do you remember the day you first met the Lord? Were you filled with joy, saying good-bye to fear? Did you feel as if a burden had been lifted off your back?

Was it like a bright spring day, with the woes of winter long gone? Did it seem as if flowers were blossoming in your heart—hope, love, peace, and patience in place of crocuses and daffodils? Was your soul suddenly like a vivid garden?

Did you imagine that birds were singing? Did you want to sing with them, praising your forgiving God?

Did you offer yourself to God fully? "All I am and all I have I give to you, Lord. After all, you have bought me with your blood." Did you say something like that?

Well, what happened? Does your heart still burn with that same flame? Or have the cold blasts of winter come back to your life? What have you done for God lately?

Would Jesus say to you what he said in Revelation: "You have forsaken your first love"?

Lord, you have blessed me so much; how can I hold back anything from you? Forgive me for being indifferent to you. Make me alive again, filled with passion for you.

43

The Price of Peace

The LORD said to Abram after Lot had parted from him, "Lift up your eyes from where you are and look north and south, east and west. All the land that you see I will give to you and your offspring forever" (Genesis 13:14–15).

Abram had just settled a family dispute. He and his nephew Lot had to divvy up the land, and he gave Lot first choice. "Let's not have any quarreling," Abram said, the words of a true peacemaker. So the God of peace blessed him. Make a note of that: If you want to stay close to God, be a person of peace.

Peace has a price. For Abram it meant giving up the best land. As a herdsman, he needed good pasture for his animals, but he let Lot take the grassiest fields. But the Lord made it up to him. "It's *all* yours, Abe. As far as you can see." Oh, sure, he had to wait a while to take possession of this land, but he had the Lord's promise.

In the same way, we have huge blessings from the promises of God. All things are ours. As children of God and heirs of the kingdom, we are zillionaires-in-waiting.

So keep the peace, and God will make it up to you.

44

Out Standing in Your Field

You will be . . . blessed in the country (Deuteronomy 28:3).

A few days ago we talked about God's blessing in the city, but he also promises to bless us in more rural areas.

Isaac was meditating in a field one night when he saw Rebekah for the first time and fell in love with her. Sometimes you have to get out in the country somewhere, alone with your thoughts and prayers, to really listen to God and know where he's leading you.

But the country isn't just for meditation. Boaz worked in the fields, overseeing a team of workers who liked and respected him. God blesses our work too.

Yes, it's true that God cursed Adam by making the soil difficult to work with, but we are blessed through the Second Adam, Jesus Christ, so we can find health and satisfaction in an honest day's work. And we give glory to God for it.

You could also go out into the country to study nature. We can learn a lot about the Creator by nosing around his creation.

Finally, people often go out to the country to bury the dead. And you too may find your "final resting place" in some rural locale. But even here we find a blessing, whether weeping at a grave or sleeping in it: Jesus is the resurrection and the life (John 11:25).

Secret Service

The LORD's unfailing love surrounds the man who trusts in him (Psalm 32:10).

When you trust in the Lord, you realize you're a sinner and you don't deserve anything. But you also know that God is brimming with unfailing love. He richly provides you with a life you know you haven't earned.

You've probably seen presidents and heads of state surrounded by their bodyguards, secret service agents assigned to keep them safe. Well, you have an even better bodyguard riding all around you—God's love! If you live in Christ Jesus, you live in the center of a system of mercy.

Right now you're surrounded by the air you breathe. But you're also surrounded by God's love. Breathe it in!

Lots of people are depressed about a lot of bad things in their lives, but God's unfailing love outweighs all those sorrows. "Rejoice in the LORD and be glad, you righteous," the psalmist says in the next verse. "Sing, all you who are upright in heart!" You don't need to bottle up your joy; let it out! As God surrounds us with his love, let us surround him with songs of thanksgiving.

46

Whatever It Takes

> The LORD remembers us and will bless us (Psalm 115:12).

He's thinking of you. He has you in mind. He remembers you and provides for you, comforts you, saves you, and guides you. The details of your life are not too trivial for him. His brain is focused on you, and it always has been. If you're concentrating on something for too long, you may need to take a break. But God never takes a break. He stays attentive to our concerns.

Because he remembers us, he will bless us. His remembering is a blessing in itself. When he thinks of us, good things happen. The verse doesn't say *how* he will bless us but just promises that he will. Even the vagueness of the promise implies that he'll do whatever it takes to bring us blessing.

So why don't we return the blessing, saying with the psalmist, "Bless the LORD, O my soul" (Psalm 103:1 KJV)!

Slammed

> I will not carry out my fierce anger, nor will I turn and devastate Ephraim. For I am God, and not man (Hosea 11:9).

Do you feel that the Lord must be angry with you right now? Are you afraid that you may turn a corner and get slammed by some judgment of God? Today's text should give you a bit of comfort.

If God shared our human sense of revenge, he would have hammered you long ago. "Stop sinning!" he'd say with a flash of anger, and you'd be toast. But that's not the way he works. "As the heavens are higher than the earth," he tells us, "so are my ways higher than your ways" (Isaiah 55:9).

You may be right: He may be angry with you. But he won't be angry forever. The Lord wants you to think about how you're living and confess your sins. If you turn back to him, he'll turn toward you. You may be up to your neck in sin, but he will shower you with forgiveness. Remember, you're not dealing with a human being here, but God. Humans would run out of patience with you, even angels might be stretched to their limit, but God is eternally patient, ready to forgive the confessing sinner.

Why not try it and see?

48

All the Way

As for you, be strong and do not give up, for your work
will be rewarded (2 Chronicles 15:7).

God had done great things for King Asa and the people
of Judah, but they were feeble folks. Their hearts were
hesitating; they weren't going all out for God.

As a result, the Lord had to give them a simple warning: "Stay with me and I'll stay with you, but leave me
behind and I'm out of here." He also reminded them of
what happened to their sister kingdom to the north, Israel. That nation had rebelled against God and was almost wiped out. When they repented, God was gracious
and gave them success.

So by warning and example God was trying to en-
courage Judah to do the right thing. Of course, the same
message applies to us. God deserves to be served with
all the energy we have.

If you're going to serve God at all, you'd better go all
the way with it. Halfhearted work isn't worth much. So
be strong and don't give up! As the New Testament tells
us, "Your labor in the Lord is not in vain" (1 Corinthians
15:58). When you throw your whole soul into it, you'll
see great things happen.

(And on a personal note, someone sent me this verse
from 2 Chronicles on a day when I was dealing with an
awful problem. It encouraged me to keep going full
speed ahead. Maybe it will do the same for you.)

49

Heart Candy

He fulfills the desires of those who fear him; he hears
their cry and saves them (Psalm 145:19).

Those who fear God are those who put him ahead of
everything else in their lives. So what do they desire? To
glorify God and enjoy him forever. God puts in our
hearts the desire for him, and then he fulfills it. When
we cry out to him, we are following the script he has
written for us.

Do you have holy desires? When people put God first,
they long to live holy lives useful to God, blessing others, honoring the Lord. Of course, they also want to have
their daily needs met. They want strength when they're
overworked, guidance when they're confused, and de-
liverance when they're in a jam. Sometimes these desires are so strong that people cry out in agony, like little children in pain, and the Lord rushes to the rescue.
"He hears their cry and saves them."

Yes, if you fear God, you have nothing else to fear. If
you cry out to the Lord, he *will* help you.

Pop this promise into your heart, like you'd pop a
piece of candy into your mouth, enjoying its sweetness
all day long.

50

Sick and Tired

> Although I have afflicted you, O Judah, I will afflict you
> no more (Nahum 1:12).

There is a limit to affliction. God sends it and God removes it.

Are you sick and tired of your troubles? Will they ever end? Remember that they will end, once and for all, when your earthly life is over. Can you patiently endure your trials until the Lord returns?

But there may be another end to your tough times. If God is disciplining you, he's waiting for you to learn your lesson. When he has whipped away your foolishness, he'll stop.

Or maybe God is testing you and wants to receive glory from the way you stay true to him even when it's difficult to do so. You wouldn't want him to stop until he got all the glory he could get, would you?

Who knows? Maybe your trials will end today. In a few hours you may be happy again. Maybe the storms of your life will subside and there will be a great calm. It's not hard for the Lord to clear the clouds from the sky.

So cheer up, will you? Sing hallelujah in anticipation of the end of your difficulties, whenever that might be.

51
24-7

The LORD will guide you always (Isaiah 58:11).

Have you lost your way? Does it seem as if you're trapped in a dense forest and can't find the path back to civilization? What should you do?

Stand still. Cry for help. See what happens. The Lord will hear your cry and will guide you. He knows the way.

Every day brings more confusion, doesn't it? Isn't it great to know that the Lord is *always* there to guide us? Of course, we can reject his advice and go our own way or look to others for guidance. But if we follow him, he will lead us 24 hours a day, 7 days a week, 365 days a year.

But look who gets this promise! Read the previous verse. "If you spend yourselves in behalf of the hungry and satisfy the needs of the oppressed . . ." We must have a heart for others, giving to the needy—and not just a few dry crusts of bread, but the kinds of things we'd like to receive. If we show concern for our fellow creatures in their time of need, God will attend to our needs and guide us always.

Jesus is not the leader of tightwads or oppressors but of the kind and tenderhearted. These are the pilgrims who will never get lost on their journey.

52

Little People

He will bless those who fear the LORD—small and great
alike (Psalm 115:13).

This is an encouraging word for anybody who feels like
a nobody. God has a big heart for little people. If you
have little money, small talent, little property, and small
influence, remember this: God cares for the small things
of creation. Even sparrows are important to him
(Matthew 10:29). Nothing is small to God. He often uses
seemingly insignificant people to accomplish his great
purposes.

The people of God include both small and great.
Some are just like newborn babies in their faith; others are giants. But all of us share God's blessing. Even
a small faith can move mountains. Even a hesitant hope
is blessed by God. The Lord Jesus bought both small
and great with the same precious blood.

There is no mother in the world who will despise her
child because it's little. On the contrary! The smaller it
is, the more tenderly she cares for it. If God has any pref-
erence at all, it is for the "least of these" (Matthew 25:45).
Notice the order in which today's verse lists them—not
"great and small," but "small and great."

53

Lions and Giants and Bears . . . Oh My!

The LORD who delivered me from the paw of the lion and the paw of the bear will deliver me from the hand of this Philistine (1 Samuel 17:37).

This is a stretch. It's not exactly one of God's promises to us, like the other verses in this book. But it has the power of a promise. David was saying what he expected to happen, and God confirmed it by making it happen.

You remember the story: The little shepherd boy David was going up against the gigantic warrior Goliath. He was arguing on past experience that God would help him in this present situation. The New Testament tells us, "No matter how many promises God has made, they are 'Yes' in Christ" (2 Corinthians 1:20), so we can claim the past experiences of David and other believers as promises for *our* present situations.

Think about the "lions and bears" you have faced in the past. There had to be situations where you came to the end of your rope, with no more power to save yourself—but God came through for you. Won't he do it again? Of course!

As David ran to meet his oversized enemy, so can you—because the Lord is with you, just as he always has been. "Never will I leave you," he says, "never will I forsake you" (Hebrews 13:5).

Why are your knees shaking before the Goliath you're facing now? Was the past just a dream? Think of the dead bear and the dead lion! True, this current problem may be different from past problems, but God is the same. He didn't get you out of your past jams only to leave you stranded in this one.

54

Remaining

If you remain in me and my words remain in you, ask whatever you wish, and it will be given you (John 15:7, emphasis added).

What does it mean to remain in Christ? It means staying in a living, loving, conscious, willing union with him, not letting other loves take his place.

In this chapter Jesus talks about himself as the vine, or the stem of a plant. We, his followers, are the branches. Now, when you look at a plant, you can see that the branches are always close to the stem—they're connected. But not only that, the branches draw their nourishment from the stem.

Yes, it's true that *all* believers remain in Christ in a sense, but this verse has a stronger meaning, which we must understand before we fully claim this promise. "Ask whatever you wish" is for people like Enoch, who "walked with God" (Genesis 5:22); for people like John, who was always at Jesus' side; for people like you, if you are in constant communication with the Lord.

Your heart must stay in love, your mind must be rooted in faith, and your hope must be cemented to Scripture. Your whole life must be connected to the Lord. Otherwise it would be too dangerous to trust us with this kind of power in prayer. This is a blank check, given only to those who know what to do with it. But if your motto is "I have been crucified with Christ and I no longer live, but Christ lives in me" (Galatians 2:20), you have his priorities.

55

Pray for Rain

> If you remain in me *and my words remain in you,* ask
> whatever you wish, and it will be given you (John 15:7,
> emphasis added).

If we want Jesus to listen to us, we must listen to him.
If we have no ear for him, he'll have no ear for us. He
pays attention to our prayers in proportion to the
amount of attention we give to his instruction.

Besides that, his words need to sink into our lives,
changing the way we think and live. In order to have
power in prayer, we need to be receptive to Jesus' teachings and to the Spirit's whispers.

But if his words do remain in us, we are in a very priv-
ileged position. We can have whatever we want, because
our wants are based on God's wants. That's how Elijah
was able to pray for rain and get it (1 Kings 18). A person like that is worth a thousand ordinary believers.

Do you really want to pray powerfully for the church
and the world? Then listen up to what Jesus is telling
you, store up his words, and make up your mind to do
what he says.

56

Running Sacred

You will be called priests of the LORD (Isaiah 61:6).

This promise was made to the Israelites, but we Christians inherit it. If we live for God, people will see it, and they'll recognize us as "priests"—people who serve the Lord. You may work or go to school, conducting your daily business like everyone else, but you'll also have another full-time job: priest. As a priest, you'll be offering sacrifices of praise, prayer, and testimony and living a holy life for God's glory.

If this is your main aim, you shouldn't be distracted so much by other concerns. Let others get caught up in politics or puzzle over finances. Let them discuss science or quibble about the arts. "Let the dead bury their own dead," Jesus said (Matthew 8:22). We are ordained to a perpetual priesthood, so let's throw ourselves into God's service.

Today's promise involves a sacred duty. Let's put on the priestly robes of holiness and do God's work all day long.

57

Truth to Tell

Truthful lips endure forever, but a lying tongue lasts only a moment (Proverbs 12:19).

Truth wears well. Time tests it, but it weathers the test. So if you're suffering right now for telling the truth, wait a while. If you believe in God's truth and try to tell others about it, you may face some opposition. But don't worry; eventually the truth will prevail.

Falsehood may triumph temporarily. It's like a plant that grows up overnight, just to die within a day. And the bigger the lie is, the harder it falls.

But truth endures forever, and this is especially true of the gospel truth, the unchanging word of our unchanging God. There's an old saying: "If you speak the truth, you shame the devil." And if you speak the truth of God, you put to shame all the lying demons of hell.

So be careful to stay on the side of truth, in big matters and in trivial things as well. More than anything, stay with the one who *is* truth (John 14:6).

58

In Suspense

He will have no fear of bad news; his heart is steadfast, trusting in the LORD (Psalm 112:7).

Let's say you're waiting for some news. A job interview, a college application, test results, a loved one in transit—what will the outcome be? Can you stand the suspense?

People may tell you, "No news is good news," but that's hard to believe. It's natural to be anxious about these things.

Faith is the cure for this condition. The Lord sends his Spirit to calm us, to banish our fear of the future.

This confidence is a great attitude to have. It's not a matter of believing in any specific promise God has made, but a general state of trust. We can be sure that God will not do us any harm or allow others to harm us. Whatever happens, we can have this confidence.

Let tomorrow come—our God is the God of tomorrow. He is the God of the known and the unknown. Come what may, we can trust the Lord. Even if the worst thing happens, our God is still the best.

So when the phone rings in the middle of the night, relax. The Lord lives! What do we have to be afraid of?

59

Play Money

You knew that you yourselves had better and lasting possessions (Hebrews 10:34).

God promises us a sweet piece of real estate in Glory Land. We can be positive about that. Put it in your portfolio. It's yours.

They say a bird in the hand is worth two in the bush, but we have both! Heaven is ours even now. We hold the title, the deposit's been paid, we even get a taste of it every so often.

How does this promise affect the way we deal with present losses? We may lose our spending money, but our treasure is safely tucked away in heaven. Our cash is just play money compared with the substantial wealth we have in Jesus, not to mention our dream home in heaven.

Better is a key word throughout the book of Hebrews. We're headed for a better land, we have a better fortune, we're given a better promise, and all this is part of a better agreement between God and us. So let's be better people, saying to the Lord, "Every day I will praise you and extol your name for ever and ever" (Psalm 145:2).

60

The Problem with Religious People

Hear the word of the LORD, you who tremble at his word: "Your brothers who hate you, and exclude you because of my name, have said, 'Let the LORD be glorified, that we may see your joy!' Yet they will be put to shame" (Isaiah 66:5).

A lot of devilish things are done in the name of God. This text is talking about good people who get mistreated by *religious* people. Because these good people are true to the Lord, they are excluded. The religious people think they're honoring God, but they're dead wrong.

Consider the bitter irony here. The devil loves the subtlety of getting his work done for supposedly religious reasons. It adds venom to the serpent's bite.

The good news is that the Lord will appear and put to shame those who are persecuting his faithful people. He'll be the defense lawyer for his chosen people, and you can bet he'll win the case.

We should be praying for all those who find themselves in this situation.

Lord, fulfill this promise! Stand up for those who are suffering for staying true to you.

61

Stealth Bombers

When you give to the needy, do not let your left hand know what your right hand is doing, so that your giving may be in secret. Then your Father, who sees what is done in secret, will reward you (Matthew 6:3–4).

There's no promise here for those who make a big show of their generosity. They're doing it to build their own reputations, and that's all the reward they'll get.

But Jesus tells us to be sneaky about our charity—even hiding it from ourselves, if you can imagine that. Give so often and so much that it's as normal as eating dinner. No big deal. Don't even bother to whisper to yourself, "Hey! I'm pretty generous!" Even that is a way of rewarding yourself. God is watching, so leave it to him to record and reward your good deed.

When it comes to giving, be a stealth bomber. Do powerful things, but keep it secret. Your private joy will be greater than worldwide recognition. The Lord will reward you—in his way, in his time, but he will reward you richly. You may not know how much he's rewarding you until you reach heaven.

So how are you going to care for the needy today, tomorrow, this week?

62

Death's Door

> You will not abandon me to the grave, nor will you let
> your Holy One see decay (Psalm 16:10).

First and foremost this verse applies to Jesus, who was
not abandoned in the grave but resurrected. In a secondary way it applies to our own resurrection, since God
promises to raise our bodies too.

But we can also read this verse in a general way. We
all have our ups and downs, and sometimes our downs
are dismal. We may feel as if we have sunk into the pit
of hell. But God won't leave us there. It may seem that
we're at death's door emotionally, mentally, even spiritually, but we won't stay there. This inner "death" will
not reach the point of utter despair. We may go very low,
but not lower than the Lord permits. We may stay in the
dankest dungeon of doubt for a while, but we won't die
there.

Even in the darkest night there's a star of hope in the
sky. The Lord won't hand us over to the enemy, so we
can relax. We're dealing with a God whose loving-
kindness endures forever! Out of our death, darkness,
and despair, we will arise to life, light, and liberty.

On Your Honor

Those who honor me I will honor (1 Samuel 2:30).

Is honoring God the whole point of your life? Does it serve as the basis for everything you do? If so, God will certainly honor you. You may go through times when people dishonor you, but God will find a way to honor you.

This verse was uttered to Eli, the priest who raised Samuel. He had dishonored the Lord by raising his sons poorly, and they were dishonoring the Lord *big time* by using their priesthood to take bribes and sleep around. So the Lord dishonored this family by taking the priesthood away from them and giving it to Samuel.

Do you want your family to be honored by God? Then honor him with your behavior. It's true that some families are honored by the world whether they deserve it or not, but God gives a special kind of honor and blessing to those who stay true to him.

What can you do today to honor the Lord? How can you speak out for him? How can you make sure you'll obey him in difficult circumstances? Can you offer your talents to serve him in some way, or give some money for his purposes? Think about how you'll honor God, because he's ready and willing to honor you.

Home Improvement

The LORD . . . blesses the home of the righteous (Proverbs 3:33).

Imagine that! The person who follows the Lord doesn't have just a personal blessing but a blessing on everyone and everything under his or her roof. A righteous home is a haven of love, a school of holy training, a place of heavenly light. Every day the Lord is honored in this home. It may be a humble cottage or a lordly mansion; it doesn't matter. The blessing is based on the character of the person who lives there, not on the square footage or market value of the home.

And it's not just mom or dad who brings the blessing on the house; a son or daughter can do this too. The Lord often protects and provides for a whole family because of one or two righteous family members. (Of course, none of us can be righteous in our own power. It's God's grace that makes us that way.)

So let's be like Mary and Martha, inviting Jesus as a regular guest in our homes. And let's try to be righteous—in our daily work or study, in our treatment of others, and in our own attitudes. A righteous God can't bless unrighteous behavior.

Show Me the Mercy!

In you the fatherless find compassion (Hosea 14:3).

When children lose their parents, the Lord steps in as a special guardian. But in the same way, when grown-ups lose friends, jobs, reputations, or opportunities—they can run to God and find what they need. This is an excellent reason for throwing away your trust in everything else and relying on God alone.

I know firsthand what it's like to hang on to the arm of God. From the evidence of my own life, I can assure you there's no other object of trust that's nearly as reliable as the ever-living God.

Some children have fathers but aren't any better off because of them. Yet everyone who has God as a father is rich. It's better to have God and no other friends than to have all the friends in the world but no God. Don't get me wrong: It's painful to be friendless or fatherless, but no one is truly abandoned if they're drinking from the Lord's fountain of mercy. If you feel bereaved or betrayed, call out to the Lord for help. The more needy and helpless you are, the more you can count on him to provide for you.

Lord, show me the mercy!

66

Unchain My Heart

The LORD sets prisoners free (Psalm 146:7).

The Lord is experienced at jailbreaks. Joseph, Jeremiah, Peter, to name a few. And God can still do this. With a word he breaks bars of brass; with a look he snaps chains of iron. He's doing it all the time—mostly in a spiritual sense. People are coming out of their spiritual slavery into the light of freedom. Jesus still throws open the doors of the heart's dungeon. Listen! Can you hear the chains jangling loose?

If you are imprisoned by sorrow, doubt, or fear, he would love to set you free. It will give him as much pleasure as it gives you. No, you don't have to break your shackles; leave that to the Emancipator. Don't get discouraged by walls of stone or bars of iron—believe in him. Satan cannot hold you, sin cannot chain you, even despair cannot bind you, if you believe right now in the Lord Jesus. Trust in his free-of-charge grace and in his awesome power.

Today's verse is your song of freedom: The Lord sets prisoners free!

Bless My Computer

Your basket and your kneading trough will be blessed (Deuteronomy 28:5).

You probably don't do a lot with a basket and kneading trough these days, but don't miss the point of this promise. These were the instruments of daily work for many of the Israelites. Farmers would gather their fruit in a basket, and bakers would knead dough to make bread. What are your instruments of daily work? The three-ring binder? The laptop computer? The broom? The forklift?

But it's not only these objects that will be blessed. When the basket is blessed, so is all the fruit inside—quite literally, the fruit of our labors. When the kneading trough is blessed, God is assuring us that he cares about our daily bread.

What is the fruit of your labor? Money, an education, a functioning home, artistic fulfillment? If you are living in obedience to God, all of this is blessed! God will make sure you earn what you need each day.

He's not saying the basket will be big. You may gather in a meager amount, living hand to mouth, getting just what you need for each day. But that's how God provided for Israel: He gave them only one day's manna at a time. What more did they need? What more do *we* need?

Lord, bless the objects of our daily work and bless what we gather in each day. Give us the power to use it all for your glory. Provide us each day what we need, and never let our savings endanger the saving of our souls.

68

Mean Cuisine

Man does not live on bread alone, but on every word that comes from the mouth of God (Matthew 4:4).

If God wanted, we could live without food. Jesus did it for forty days. But we can't live without God's word. By his word we were created (John 1:3), and we are kept alive by it. Food is a secondary matter next to the importance of God's word.

It's great to feed the hungry, and it's good to pray for our own daily bread, but let's not lock God into one way of working. Some Christians have reported that when they were so poor they couldn't afford to eat, they had less of an appetite. God can work that way too. It's natural for us to pay attention to visible needs, but let's keep our focus on the invisible God.

Communication with God is more important than food. We *must* have it. We need it to resist the devil (as Jesus did when he uttered today's verse). We need it to feed our souls. All the books and sermons in the world cannot provide us with a single meal—apart from the word of the Lord. This is the cuisine we cannot do without.

Lord, feed us with your word. Let's keep the lines of communication open.

Daylight

I have come into the world as a light, so that no one who believes in me should stay in darkness (John 12:46).

This world is as gloomy as midnight. Jesus has come to brighten our lives.

No one is a huge concept. Not you. Not me. *Nobody* has to sit in the shadow of death, as long as he or she trusts in Jesus. Believers can walk out into the light of a day that will never end. What are you waiting for?

Dark clouds will come along from time to time, but we won't stay in darkness if we believe in Jesus. He comes to give us broad daylight. Our nighttime was full of ignorance, doubt, despair, sin, fear, and a nasty tendency to do exactly the wrong thing—but Jesus came to set us free from all that. Faith brings us the privilege of sunlight; let's enjoy it.

Yes, shake off your depression, my friend. Move out of the dark and into the light. Your hope, your joy, your paradise is in Jesus. Pay attention to him. Trust only in him. Then you'll be able to sing with the birds as they welcome the rising sun—and with the angels as they praise the risen Son.

Grab Your Slingshot!

> All those gathered here will know that it is not by sword or spear that the LORD saves; for the battle is the LORD's, and he will give all of you into our hands (1 Samuel 17:47).

The battle you're fighting is the Lord's battle, and he's going to win. You can book it. He will find the best way to display his power, and he'll do it.

People forget about God. They get so wrapped up in their struggles that they ignore God's hand in their lives. If Israel could forget their God, anyone can! They were counting on swords and spears to defeat their enemies, but David walked out to fight the giant Goliath with no spear in his hand. All he had was the confidence that God would win.

If you are truly fighting for truth and justice, don't wait until you've gathered all the visible wealth or talent or power you think you need. Grab a few stones from the brook, get your slingshot ready, and go out to meet the enemy. That's a crazy strategy if you're fighting your own battle, but if you're standing up for Jesus and relying on his strength, who's going to beat you? Don't hesitate! If the almighty Lord is with us, who can be against us (Romans 8:31)?

Going Out

About Zebulun he said: "Rejoice, Zebulun, in your going out" (Deuteronomy 33:18).

As Christians we can claim the promises of the tribes of Israel, for we are their spiritual heirs. Zebulun would find joy in "going out," and so will we—but what does this mean?

We go out when we travel, and the Lord protects us. For some, going out is moving to a new home, and the Lord goes before us, preparing the way. Some go out as missionaries, and Jesus promised the first missionaries, "Surely I am with you always, to the very end of the age" (Matthew 28:20). Every day, we go out to work or school, and we can rejoice that God will be with us from morning to night.

Sometimes when we start out on a trip, a sense of fear creeps over us. What will happen to us? What will we find along the way? But today's verse can reassure us, so take it with you wherever you go (at least in your memory). You can sing with joy whenever you board a plane or just hop into a car; we belong to the rejoicing tribe, and every going out is an opportunity to praise God.

Childproof

"Ah, Sovereign LORD," I said, "I do not know how to speak; I am only a child." But the LORD said to me, "Do not say, 'I am only a child.' You must go to everyone I send you to and say whatever I command you" (Jeremiah 1:6–7).

Can you imagine what Jeremiah was thinking? He felt so young and insignificant, but God was giving him a great errand to do. Gulp. How could he possibly succeed?

Was Jeremiah just being humble? Maybe, but it doesn't matter, because he had been chosen to speak *God's* message. Jeremiah didn't have to make up brilliant things to say or market himself to get good ratings. All he had to do was follow orders: say what God wanted, when God wanted. God would give him the ability.

What message has God given you to express to others? Are you leading a Bible study group, teaching a class, or perhaps sharing your faith with a friend? God knows exactly how young you are, how slim your knowledge is, how little experience you have. But if he chooses to entrust you with his message, how can you say no? God will magnify himself in your weakness.

If you were as old as Methuselah, how would that help you? If you were as wise as Solomon, you might be just as willful as he turned out to be. Stay with the message God gives you; that's all the wisdom you need.

God Is like Mom

As a mother comforts her child, so will I comfort you (Isaiah 66:13).

This is the very picture of tenderness. A mother enters into her child's sadness, hugging so tightly she could almost transplant the little one's grief into her own heart. A child can tell a mother anything, and the mother will sympathize as nobody else can. Mothers are generally the best comforters, and even full-grown adults have found this true of their elderly moms.

We often think of God as our Father, but is he a Mother to us as well? Today's verse says yes. As the Comforter, God brings us into a holy familiarity with himself, a confidence in his strength, a sacred relaxation.

We can tell God about our troubles, even through sobs and sighs. Mothers don't mind tears and neither does God. As a mother understands her child's weaknesses, so God understands us, but he also helps us get rid of our faults in a way no mother ever could.

It would be unfair to God if we tried to carry our sorrow alone. He is gentle and kind, waiting to console us. And as mothers never seem to get tired of holding their babies in their arms, so God never gets tired of us. We can start each day with him and stay close to him all day long.

Far from Home

This is what the Sovereign LORD says: Although I sent them far away among the nations and scattered them among the countries, yet for a little while I have been a sanctuary for them in the countries where they have gone (Ezekiel 11:16).

Do you feel like a foreigner? Does it seem as if you don't belong in your community, in your school, in your job, in this world? That's the way it is for many believers, and if that's your story, today's promise is for you.

The scattered Jews were bemoaning the fact that they could no longer worship in the temple in Jerusalem, but the Lord promised to be a sanctuary for them and a home for everyone who feels far from home.

God is a place of protection. No matter what enemy is chasing us down, we can find sanctuary with him. God is our place of worship too. Long before tabernacles or temples, Jacob slept in a field and woke up saying, "Surely the LORD is in this place" (Genesis 28:16). God is also a place of peace and quiet, like the innermost part of the temple, shut off from the hectic and harried noises of this world.

In Jesus Christ we also find a place of mercy. The temple housed the ark of the covenant, the symbol of God's relationship with his people. But through Christ we are forgiven and welcomed by God, so God is also our place of communion as we celebrate our relationship with God. What more do we need?

O Lord, be our home away from home.

Do As I Do

Whatever you have learned or received or heard from me, or seen in me—put it into practice. And the God of peace will be with you (Philippians 4:9).

It's great when someone can say that: "Follow my example." Paul, who wrote these words, was well aware that he got his strength from Christ (see Philippians 4:13), and that's our power source too.

If we manage to put Paul's teachings into practice, we can claim the promise—and what an amazing promise it is! God, who loves peace and makes peace and *breathes* peace—this God of peace will be with us.

In some churches they "pass the peace" as part of the service, saying, "Peace be with you" to one another. But this promise involves far more. We have the fountain as well as the streams, the sun as well as the beams. If the God of peace is with us, we can enjoy his peace, which goes beyond all human understanding (see Philippians 4:7). Even if circumstances go totally wacky on us, threatening to disturb our peace of mind, we still have the peace of God. If fights break out all around us, we can be peacemakers, because the God of peace is with us.

True peace is found in the way of truth. Don't try to push for peace by ditching your faith or ignoring God's call to live a holy life. That would be a bad mistake. Be pure first, then peaceful. Stick to the teachings we get from Paul, and the God of peace will go with you.

No Fear

"Do not be afraid of them, for I am with you and will rescue you," declares the LORD (Jeremiah 1:8).

When fear makes us falter, we're in danger of falling into sin. You don't want to be conceited, but you don't want to be cowardly either. Christ needs brave soldiers in his army.

And we have reason to be confident, because God promises to be with us. God won't call in sick on the day of battle. He'll be there.

What do you have to be afraid of? Say your life is in danger. So? You've got a new life ahead of you.

Will you lose your job? Does your entire future rest on this one boss or teacher or coach who never liked you anyway? God will take care of your needs. Can't you trust him?

Are you afraid people will make fun of you? Jesus knows what that's about. He'll help you deal with it and even rejoice.

Remember how Daniel came out of the lions' den un-bitten and how his three friends stepped out of the fire unburned. You're probably not facing situations quite so serious, but even if you were, God would steer you safely through.

Be afraid to be afraid. Your worst enemy is your own heart pounding in terror, or perhaps your knees knocking away. Use those knees to pray for help, and then stand up again, saying, "I will trust in God, and I won't be afraid."

Pray As You Go

The prayer of the upright pleases him (Proverbs 15:8).

God loves it when good people pray. But what does it mean to be good—or "upright," as this verse puts it? It means that we live life straight up, not crooked with corruption or bowing down to evil. Nor do we veer off in bad directions. We are straightforward in our dealings with others. We act with integrity.

If you try crooked ways, you'll find that praying is practically impossible. It'll feel as if your prayers were splattering on the ceiling, never quite making it to heaven.

So are you living in a straight line, as the Lord wants? Are you upright? If so, pray all you can. If this is what God delights in, let's not cheat him out of a moment.

God doesn't care about your grammar or your metaphysical theories or your speaking ability. Other people might grade you on these things, but not the Lord. He takes pleasure in the lispings of his children, in the stammerings of his newborn sons and daughters. And if this pleases the Lord so much, shouldn't we delight in it too? Let's go to God's throne as often as we can. The Lord gives us plenty of reasons to pray—we ought to thank him for that.

78

Grace under Fire

The LORD will give grace and glory (Psalm 84:11 KJV).

We need grace right now, and it's available to us free of charge. What can be freer than a gift? And that's exactly what grace is: a gift of God's favor. Today you will receive his warm smiles, his strong arms, his rich laughter, his comforting voice! It's all there for the taking.

The Lord never says, "Sorry, I'm all out of grace. Got a shipment coming in next Thursday. Try me again later." You want grace? He's got grace and plenty of it. Take all you want.

Now, we're not talking about money. God won't make you rich, at least not in the way most people define wealth. He won't pad your bank account, but his grace is far more valuable than that. Sometimes he will even make things difficult for you, but he'll always give you the grace you need to get through.

There's a great *and* in today's verse. God promises to give us grace *and* glory. We don't need glory yet—in fact, we aren't ready for it yet—but we will have it when the time comes. Once we've eaten the bread of grace, we'll drink the wine of glory. Grace makes us holy, and then there is glory. Those little words *and glory* are enough to make me dance for joy. Want to join me?

Just a little while longer, and then we'll have glory forever!

79

Designer Clothes

If that is how God clothes the grass of the field, which is here today and tomorrow is thrown into the fire, will he not much more clothe you, O you of little faith? (Matthew 6:30).

Clothes are expensive, and if you're tight on funds, you might worry about how you'll pay for your next outfit. Your sneakers are getting grungy, but can you afford new Nikes?

God's way ahead of you. He decks out the grass in green finery—so why can't he clothe his own children? You can bet that he will. It may take some patching and darning and a commitment to thrift-store fashion, but he'll take care of you.

I know a poor minister whose clothes were nearly threadbare, literally falling apart at the seams. Yet he trusted God to provide his clothing. On a visit to the area, I served as the guest speaker in this man's church, and it suddenly occurred to me that I should take up a collection for this minister's needs. *Voila!* There was his new wardrobe.

I've seen many other cases like this, in which God provides clothing to those who need it. If you think back to the beginning of clothing, you'll remember that Adam and Eve were ashamed because of their sin, but God provided clothes for them. And the skins he gave them were far finer than the leaves they sewed for themselves.

80

Travel Plans

You will go on your way in safety, and your foot will not stumble (Proverbs 3:23).

If you stay in the path of wisdom and holiness, you'll travel safely. It only makes sense: Travel in daylight is safer than travel at night, and if you have to go at night, it's best to stay on the main highway. So stay in God's light and in his path.

Every person has his or her own travel plans in life— I'm talking about what God has called you to do. If you stay in that plan, God will preserve you from evil. It won't always be a comfy trip, but it will be safe.

The biggest problem lies with us: We stumble very easily. We need to ask God for more moral strength so we can overcome our tendency to slip. Some stumble because they don't see the obstacles they trip over. God can help us to see sin for what it is, so we can learn to avoid it. Let's ask him for this help and trust him to provide it.

Wouldn't it be great to go through this entire day without stumbling, without even the smallest misstep? You can if you keep your focus on the God who promises to protect you.

81

Grateful for Grace

God . . . gives grace to the humble (James 4:6).

Humble hearts seek grace, so they get it. Humble people respond to God's grace, letting it shape their lives—and that's why God gives them more and more of it. When you're humble, you're not on some mountaintop crowing about yourself; you're in the valley, and that's where the streams of grace are flowing. You can drink your fill. Humility makes you grateful for God's grace, so you praise God for it. God likes to be praised, so of course he's going to heap more grace upon you.

Be humble, then. Don't make too much of yourself—let God do that for you.

"Oh no!" you might say. "I'm not very humble at all." That, my friend, is the true language of humility. Some people are proud of being humble, and that's the worst kind of pride. We are needy, helpless creatures deserving only hell, and if we aren't humble, we ought to be.

So it's good to be humble, even about your humility. It's only God's grace that makes us humble, and he takes advantage of our humility to pour more grace upon us. So let's go downward so God can lift us upward. Let's be poor in spirit so God can make us rich. If we humble ourselves, God won't have to humble us, but by his grace he'll exalt us.

82

Seeing Eye God

I will lead the blind by ways they have not known (Isaiah 42:16).

You may find this scandalous, but get the picture: God is acting as a Seeing Eye dog. I know it's tough to see the infinitely glorious God in such humble terms, but that's the image we have here.

Blind people can't find their way on roads they don't know. Even familiar roads are difficult for them; new roads are out of the question. So if we're talking about the road to salvation, all of us are blind by nature. We don't know the way—unless the Lord takes our hands, leads us along, and eventually opens our eyes.

In the same way, we're traveling a road into the future, and we have no clue as to what's going to happen. But the Lord Jesus will lead us. Thank God!

We don't know how God is going to rescue us from future predicaments, but we know he'll be there beside us every step of the way. We can relax when we take his hand, trusting him to lead us safely home. Someday we'll get to our eternal home and our eyes will finally be opened, and we will launch into a major song of gratitude to the Guide who walked with us.

Lord, I have to admit, I don't know where I'm going. Lead me today.

83

Stupid People

The Lord is faithful, and he will strengthen and protect you from the evil one (2 Thesssalonians 3:3).

Sometimes people aren't just evil, they're stupid. There's no use arguing with them or trying to make peace. They have false hearts and deceitful words. What can we do about these people? Should we worry about them?

No. We must turn to the Lord. When people are faithless, he is faithful. When people break their promises, he always keeps his. When people make unreasonable demands on us, he is always reasonable. In a back-stabbing world, we can rejoice in the embrace of our honest God.

He will strengthen us so we can stand up against the attacks of evil people, those whose actions are inspired by the evil one. God will protect us from the damage these people try to do to us. This is a great blessing in a dog-eat-dog world. We can find shelter in Jesus, who sympathizes with our situation.

There is one true heart, one faithful mind, one never changing love. Let's rest there, in Jesus. He will fulfill his purposes within us, no matter what evil people may do to us.

Lord, strengthen and protect me from evil!

Dream Keeper

When you lie down, you will not be afraid; when you lie down, your sleep will be sweet (Proverbs 3:24).

When you go to bed at night, this promise can smooth your pillow. You can't keep watch over yourself as you sleep, but God can. Those who lie down with God's protection are safer than kings and queens in their palaces, with all their bodyguards.

Try this: When you lie down in bed, lay down your worries and ambitions. If you do, you'll sleep much better than anxious and covetous people do. Bad dreams will be banished—or at least you'll know they're only dreams.

Peter was in prison, about to be put to death, but he was sleeping so soundly he didn't wake up when the angel's light filled his cell. The angel had to give him a jab in the ribs (Acts 12:7). Other Christians have died for their faith, but they didn't lose any sleep over it. "He grants sleep to those he loves" (Psalm 127:2).

If you want to sleep soundly, try living soundly, praying steadily, and loving solidly.

85

The God Who Cares

The LORD will sustain him on his sickbed and restore him from his bed of illness (Psalm 41:3).

Here's another great promise, but when we look at the context, we see it's given to those who care for the poor. Are you one of these?

See how tender this picture is. The everlasting arms of the almighty God will hold up the soul of this sick person just as friendly hands and downy pillows prop up his body. This is a God who sympathizes, who sits next to us in our sorrow. What other gods of the world are shown like this? Jove, the king of the Roman gods, wouldn't be caught dead in this scene. Are the gods of India or China any more sympathetic?

No, this word picture is unique to the God of Israel. Only he volunteers to serve as nursemaid to the sick. Sure, he's still the almighty God, but if he disciplines us with one hand, he comforts us with the other.

Grace is the best medicine. Seriously, God's love is the best treatment possible for the ailing soul. It makes the soul as strong as a football lineman, even if the body is wasting away. There's no doctor like the Lord, no vitamins like his promise, no diet like his love.

So if you're not active in helping the poor, see what you're missing. Get with it!

86

Here Am I!

Come near to God and he will come near to you (James 4:8).

The nearer we get to God, the more intimate he gets with us. When the prodigal son returns to his father, the father rushes out to meet him. When the wandering dove returns to the ark, Noah stretches out his hand to bring the bird back home. It's the same way with God. He's waiting for you to get close to him.

Did you ever notice that phrase in Isaiah 58:9: "Then you will call, and the LORD will answer; you will cry for help, and he will say: *Here am I*"? With those three words, the Lord seems to put himself at the disposal of his people, like the clerk at the corner store—"What can I do for you?"

What are you waiting for? God is ready to forgive, to bless, to comfort, to help, to energize, to rescue. The one thing you need to do is get close to him. Once you do that, you're set. If you get close to others, they may get tired of you eventually and leave you, but the Lord is different. If you get tight with him, he will come closer and closer to you in a beautiful friendship that knows no limits.

87

Heads or Tails?

The LORD will make you the head, not the tail (Deuteronomy 28:13).

Heads or tails?

Today's strange promise comes from God's Old Testament blessings to those who obey him. "Follow me," he says, "and I'll put you at the head of the class."

Believers should be leading the march through life, not tagging along afterward. We should be influencing people for good, not being dragged here and there by others. We must not give in to the spirit of our age but convince the people of this age to honor Christ.

In another part of Scripture it says that God has made us priests. Well, priests teach, and we can teach the ways of the Lord to those around us. We don't need to be learning the tactics of unbelievers. God intends for us to rule the earth—so how can we be servants of custom, slaves of human opinion?

Have you taken a stand for Jesus? Too many people stay silent because they're afraid to speak up or perhaps because they just don't care. Should we allow the name of the Lord Jesus to be kept in the background? Should our faith be dragged along like a tail? No way. Our faith should be at the head of our lives, illuminating a path for others.

88

Still as Stone

I am with you, and no one is going to attack and harm you (Acts 18:10).

God had work for Paul to do in the city of Corinth, so he gave him this promise. There was a riot in the streets, but no one could stop the preaching of the gospel or the conversion of those who heard it. God has power even over the most violent minds. As the Israelites, after passing through the Red Sea, said of their enemies: "By the power of your arm they will be as still as a stone—until your people pass by" (Exodus 15:16).

So if you are doing what God wants, you don't need to be afraid of what people might do to you. Stay on course. I'm not saying that you'll never face some terrifying situations; you may. But faith in God brushes fear away like cobwebs. No one can harm us unless the Lord allows it, and the Lord will only allow what's best for us. The Lord can drive the devil away with a single word, and he certainly has power over the devil's agents. In fact, they may be more afraid of you than you are of them.

So go forward, completing the task God has given you, and where you expected to find enemies, you may find friends.

89

Pray for Keeps

> Do not be anxious about anything, but in everything, by prayer and petition, with thanksgiving, present your requests to God. And the peace of God, which transcends all understanding, will guard your hearts and your minds in Christ Jesus (Philippians 4:6–7).

No care, just prayer. No anxiety, just joyful friendship with God. Carry your concerns to the Lord of your life, the guardian of your soul. Make the mixture two parts prayer to one part praise. Don't pray doubtfully; pray thankfully. Assume that God is already giving you what you've asked for and thank him for that. Don't hide anything. Don't let any desire lie festering in your heart; present your requests. Don't run to other people to get your needs met; go to God.

And the result? God's peace. You won't understand it, but you'll have it. God's peace will fold you in a sweet embrace. Your heart and mind will bathe in a sea of rest. No matter what happens to you—poverty, pain, lying friends, even death—you will live with Jesus above it all. Why not go to God with your needs and concerns?

Lord, I do believe you. But help me believe you more.

90

Ready for Anything

Have no fear of sudden disaster or of the ruin that overtakes the wicked, for the LORD will be your confidence and will keep your foot from being snared (Proverbs 3:25–26).

We need three things.

1. Courage. We have the presence of God, so we ought to display presence of mind. When disasters occur suddenly, we shouldn't be surprised. After all, we expect the Lord to return at any moment; we should be ready for anything. If we can stay serene during major crises, that's a precious gift from God.

2. Discernment. What is going on here? Is the world coming to an end? Is there a natural disaster? Or is God punishing the wicked? If the current calamity is punishment, we need to recognize it as a good remedy for bad sin. We should be far more upset about the sin that deserves hell than about the hell that results from sin.

3. Peace. If the Lord is our confidence, we'll trust in his protection. Satan and his whole team are trying to trip us up, but the Lord will guard our path. We won't fall for their tricks.

So go on if you believe in Jesus. Let the Lord be your confidence, and greet each day with courage, discernment, and peace—no matter what may happen.

91

Going Straight

A highway will be there; it will be called the Way of Holiness. The unclean will not journey on it; it will be for those who walk in that Way; wicked fools will not go about on it (Isaiah 35:8).

The Way of Holiness is so straight that even the dumbest people can't go wrong if they just stay on the road. It's the worldly-wise people who get into trouble. They keep making twists and turns, trusting their own judgment, but they usually make terrible mistakes.

When people make their decisions according to the world's priorities, they're shortsighted. They may seem smart at the time, but those decisions just lead people off the road, making them lose their way.

On the other hand, people of faith just do what God tells them. They stay on God's road, under his protection.

Are you in a jam? How can you get out? Tell a lie? Do something that God won't like? Forget about it! Stay in the middle of God's road, the road of truth and integrity— that's your best course of action. Stop going around in circles. Practice justice in all your relationships, and you won't have to worry. Stay straight on God's superhighway, following Jesus. What can go wrong?

Even if you could get out of a jam by doing something wrong, you'd just fall into a worse predicament by doing that bad thing. God's way is the best way. People may think you're silly for following it, but you're actually the wise one.

Lord, keep me on your straight highway.

92

Wholly Holy

Be diligent in these matters; give yourself wholly to them, so that everyone may see your progress (1 Timothy 4:15).

When we invest ourselves in the work of God, the pay-off will be obvious to everyone. We're not talking about a speed-reading of Scripture, but deep meditation on it. Not busywork for God, but our best work. Not a lot of fuss and hurry with slovenly results, but the loving energy of our whole souls.

You can't split your efforts between God and money or between Christ's glory and your own. Give yourself wholly to holiness. Otherwise you're like the stock trader who can't make up his mind. Buy! Or maybe sell! Whatever! At the final bell, while others count their profits, you're empty-handed.

Are you a servant of God? Then go for it! Why waste your time on party politics or cheap entertainment? Make your commitment to Jesus the most important thing in your life—your job, your calling, your single pursuit. Go out and out for Jesus (after going in and in with him in your heart). Otherwise you'll see no progress or profit, and the world will miss out on the powerful influence you could have.

93

Global Warning

Because your heart was responsive and you humbled yourself before the LORD when you heard what I have spoken against this place and its people, that they would become accursed and laid waste, and because you tore your robes and wept in my presence, I have heard you, declares the LORD (2 Kings 22:19).

A lot of people get warned by God and ignore it. They also suffer for it. The smart person takes God's warnings seriously.

In today's verse it's the young King Josiah who has heard God's word and responded. God was going to bring judgment on the nation of Judah for their sinful ways, but he was moved by Josiah's repentance.

How responsive are you? Do you humble yourself and repent when God calls some sin to your attention? If so, God will spare you. God knows which people are sighing and crying over the sins of their culture. When the destroying angel comes to exact God's judgment, it passes by the chosen ones, those with humble, responsive hearts.

Are you troubled by the sins of the world? Do you fear that God will judge your nation harshly? You may have good reason. But if you remain responsive to God, you can claim the promise that Josiah got: "You will be buried in peace. Your eyes will not see all the disaster I am going to bring on this place" (2 Kings 22:20). Better still, the Lord Jesus may return for us, and our days of mourning will be over.

94

Hornets Win!

I will send the hornet ahead of you to drive the Hivites,
Canaanites and Hittites out of your way (Exodus 23:28).

The hornets acted as God's own army, forcing people
out of the land that God promised to Israel, making it
easier for the Israelites to settle in Canaan. God fights
for his people in his own ways. Sure, sometimes he uses
people to fight for him, but often there are strange,
miraculous forces that get the job done.

So we have nothing to fear. The air itself will fight for
us. The stars in their courses are part of our supporting
army. Sometimes we'll get all ready for some conflict
and find no one to do battle with! As the Bible says, "The
LORD will fight for you; you need only to be still" (Exodus 14:14). God's hornets can do more than our
weapons. He wins battles in ways we can't even dream
of.

Yes, we are given marching orders. In a way, we are
part of God's army, called to fight for him. But we often
find that God has gone before us, fighting for us, preparing the way. In the final analysis, "It was not by their
sword that they won the land, nor did their arm bring
them victory; it was your right hand, your arm, and the
light of your face, for you loved them" (Psalm 44:3).

95

God's Amnesia

I have made you, you are my servant; O Israel, I will not forget you (Isaiah 44:21).

Our God cannot forget his servants. He has chosen us not for a short time but for forever, and he'll never stop loving us. He already knew what we would be when he adopted us into his family. He blots out our sins, and he will never condemn us for sins that he's blotted out.

He will not forget his people. If he did stop thinking of us, even for a moment, it would be disastrous for us. We may forget other people and they may forget us. Even people we have helped in the past may forget us in the future. It happens. We can't count on having a permanent place in human hearts, but God will not forget us. And that's not because of anything we've done for him but because of what he's done for us. He has loved us for too long to forget us; he has bought us with too high a price. Jesus knows the pain he went through to win us, and he cannot forget. The Father sees us as the bride of his Son, and the Spirit sees his own work within us. None of that is easy to forget.

With all that in mind, how can we forget the Lord?

96

Fantastic Future

> The LORD will be king over the whole earth. On that day there will be one LORD, and his name the only name (Zechariah 14:9).

Fantastic! But it's not just a fantasy. God promises that he will rule the world and that every nation will acknowledge his power. You can be sure it will happen.

Of course, we don't see that today. Where do we see anybody bowing before the great King? We see a lot of rebellion, a lot of false gods, a lot of people grabbing for their own power. Even among Christians there are all sorts of strange ideas about Jesus and the gospel message. But one day there will be one King, one Lord, one name for the living God! I hope it comes soon.

Now, let's not get all wrapped up in a discussion of when this will happen. That may take away from our joy in the fact that it will happen. Jesus did not die in vain. The Spirit doesn't work in vain. The Father's eternal plans will take place. Here on earth, where Satan once triumphed, Jesus will be crowned king, and the all-powerful God will reign. This has to make you feel good as you go about your daily activities. It isn't over till it's over!

O Lord, your kingdom come!

97

My Bodyguard

All the peoples on earth will see that you are called by the name of the LORD, and they will fear you (Deuteronomy 28:10).

Why then are we afraid of *them?* God can make us so much like himself that it will be obvious to those around us that we belong to him. He's waiting to do this for us.

You can be sure of this: Ungodly people have a fear of true Christ-followers. They may hate them, but they fear them too. In fact, their hate often arises out of fear, though they're too proud to admit it.

So let's trip along the path of truth without terror. Fear is not for us but for those who fight against the almighty Lord. If we are truly called by the name of the Lord, that's a great insurance policy. A few thousand years ago a Roman citizen merely had to say, *"Romanus sum"*—"I am a Roman"—and he could claim the protection of all the armies of that vast empire. Our situation is even better. If you can say, "I am a Christian," you have the all-powerful God as your bodyguard—and God would rather empty heaven of angels than leave a Christian without protection.

98

Witness Protection Program

> The following night the Lord stood near Paul and said, "Take courage! As you have testified about me in Jerusalem, so you must also testify in Rome" (Acts 23:11).

Are you in danger of some kind because you have testified about the Lord? Well, God has a fabulous witness protection program. If he has more people for you to talk to, he'll keep you going until you do. No one's going to snuff out God's candle.

That assurance should help you relax a bit, and it might kick you in the pants too. You are a witness for Jesus in the trial of the century—the trial of the millennium!—and your major concern should be the quality and truthfulness of your testimony.

People may try to discredit you, telling harmful lies about you. Your friends may desert you or betray you. But whatever happens, God has a purpose for you. "You *must* testify," God says. That's an offer you can't refuse.

You may not need this promise right now, but you may need it soon, so pack it away for future use. And in the meantime, remember to pray for missionaries and persecuted Christians all around the world, that God would protect them as they offer their testimony.

Calming the Storm

Great peace have they who love your law, and nothing can make them stumble (Psalm 119:165).

Yep, a true love for the Good Book will bring us great peace from an awesome God. It will also be a solid source of protection. If you check in regularly with what God is saying, it will keep your stress levels down. The Holy Spirit is your Comforter, your Counselor, speaking through Scripture, calming the storms in your soul.

If the Word of God camps out in your heart, you don't stumble through life. Instead, your daily experiences become a thrilling adventure. Sure, there are trials, tough times of testing, but they don't get you down. God's warnings help you anticipate them, and they don't seem so surprising when they arrive.

Many people stumble when they go through good times, times of wealth and success. But if you love what God tells you, you'll stay on your feet in fortune and failure, because you'll be living beyond your changing circumstances.

And when others are troubled by some mystery of the faith, you'll accept it. Any intellectual difficulties are overcome by your reverent awe of God's Word.

Lord, give us this great peace today.

100

Look and Live

The LORD said to Moses, "Make a snake and put it up on a pole; anyone who is bitten can look at it and live" (Numbers 21:8).

What a great picture of Jesus!

Jesus, a snake? Well, yes. Go with me on this.

Jesus was considered a criminal, and he was hung up on a pole—that is, a cross. And anyone who looks at him—that is, comes to meet him—will be healed of the snakebite of sin. Get it?

If you're feeling as if sin has taken a bite out of you, listen to these words: "Anyone who is bitten can look at it and live." *Anyone!* I found it true in my own life: I looked to Jesus and immediately had new life. If you look to Jesus, you will live too. You may feel as if you're already swelling up with the snake's venom and there's no hope for you. The truth is, there's only one hope: looking to Jesus.

The bronze serpent that Moses lifted up in the desert was not just a decoration for healthy people to admire. It was there to save sick people! In the same way, Jesus died as a real Savior for real sinners. The bite of sin may have made you a drug addict, a thief, or a sex fiend—it doesn't matter. A look at the Savior will heal you, bringing you into a healthy relationship with God.

Look and live.

101

Know Way!

"No longer will a man teach his neighbor, or a man his brother, saying, 'Know the LORD,' because they will all know me, from the least of them to the greatest," declares the LORD (Jeremiah 31:34).

There's an awful lot we don't know, but we do know the Lord. This is a promise that we have already seen fulfilled, and it's not a trivial matter. Even the least believer among us knows God, through Christ Jesus. Not as much as we want to, of course, but we really know him! We don't just know doctrines about him; we know *him*. He is our Father and our Friend. We have a personal relationship with him. We can say, "My Lord and my God" (John 20:28). We are on a first-name basis with him, and we spend lots of time in his company.

How did this relationship start? Did we ourselves figure out how to meet God? No way. It was God who broke through the universe and introduced himself to us. He is the source of this knowledge of him. He is the fountain of all saving knowledge.

To know God is eternal life. When we first came to meet him, he energized us. He has raised us to newness of life. So let's praise him all day long, and let's keep getting to know him even better.

102

Sin? What Sin?

I will forgive their wickedness and will remember their sins no more (Jeremiah 31:34).

When we know the Lord, we get our sins forgiven. We know him as the God of grace, the one who accepts us in spite of our crimes.

But notice how this promise is worded: The Lord will remember our sins no more. Can God forget? That's what he says here—and he means what he says. He will treat us as if we had never sinned! Christ's sacrifice wiped out our sin so completely that it doesn't even exist in God's mind anymore. As God sees it, the believer is as innocent as Adam and Eve were before their sin—in fact, more so, because we have *God's* righteousness and not just our own.

Our great Lord forgets our sins. That means he can't punish us for them, nor can he love us any less because of them. Once a debt is paid, it stops being a debt. In the same way, God has cleared the books for his people.

Do you feel guilty about your sins and shortcomings? If that motivates you to improve your behavior, all right, but rest assured that God will never bring them up against you. And God's free pardon makes us want to please him by staying obedient.

103

Body Work

[He] will transform our lowly bodies so that they will be like his glorious body (Philippians 3:21).

Does your body ever feel lowly? Maybe it's when you're in terrible pain or so sick you think you're going to die. Maybe it's when you see yourself in a mirror and wish you were taller, thinner, shapelier, stronger. Or maybe your body seems lowliest when it leads you into temptation—fueled by its desire for sex or drugs or food or some other pleasure. Our bodies can truly humble us.

But our Savior, Jesus, will change all that. Everyone who trusts in Jesus will get a body like his body. Since our souls have been transformed, it only makes sense that we'd get a body to match. When? We don't know. But the thought of it should keep us going.

In a little while we'll be the way Jesus is now. No more pounding headaches, no more sprained ankles, no more hormones pushing us to do the wrong thing. Our bodies will be like his glorious body. A promise like that can give us hope even when we feel most hopeless.

104

Fire Yourself

He chose our inheritance for us (Psalm 47:4).

Can you think of anyone better to make that choice? If your enemies chose your inheritance, it would be a sad one. But even if you chose your own, it wouldn't be nearly as splendid as what God has in store for you. A wiser mind than yours is arranging your destiny. Would you want it any other way?

Knowing how easily we mess things up for ourselves, we should be glad to let God decide our destiny. We're safer with him in the driver's seat than we could ever be if we were behind the wheel. We can feel good about leaving our painful present and unknown future in the hands of our Father, our Savior, our Comforter.

If you've been making your own decisions lately, ignoring God's directions, it's time to turn the reins of your life over to God. Fire yourself as your own CEO and let the Lord call the shots. Make the choice to let him make the choices. Yes, you're a free agent; you can decide what you want. But doesn't it make tons of sense to leave it up to God?

105

Ask Large

What the righteous desire will be granted (Proverbs 10:24).

Because it is a righteous desire, it is safe for God to grant it. It wouldn't be any good for God to give the unrighteous their desires, since there's no telling what they'd want. That might be a disaster for society and for the desirers themselves. But if we keep the Lord's commands, he will pay close attention to what we ask for.

But what if righteous people desire unrighteous things? Well then, all bets are off, because these are not their real desires. They're wanderings or blunders, and they deserve to be refused. But when we bring our truly righteous desires to God, he will not say no.

But doesn't God sometimes hear our requests and say, "Not yet"? Yes, but today's promise should inspire us to ask again. Doesn't he sometimes give us a flat-out no? If so, we should still thank him, because don't we want him to say no when he knows that's better for us?

Yet we can be very bold in asking for some things.

"I want to be holy, Lord."

"Use me for your glory."

"Make me more like Christ."

"Prepare me for heaven."

These desires come from the grace of God within us—we'd never ask them on our own—and we can be sure that God will not hold back on these requests. So in these matters, ask large!

As the psalmist says, "Delight yourself in the LORD and he will give you the desires of your heart" (Psalm 37:4).

106

Property of Jesus

On that day HOLY TO THE LORD will be inscribed on the bells of the horses (Zechariah 14:20).

What a great day that will be when everything is holy, even the horses' bells!

But isn't that day here already? It could be. Think about it. Can't you make the things in your life holy to the Lord?

When you put on your clothes, won't that remind you of the righteousness of Jesus, which you put on to stand before the Father? When you do your work, isn't that also for the Lord? Every day, your clothes can be like holy robes, your meals like communion, your words like incense. Your house can be a temple, your desk an altar, and you a priest.

If you want this, if you believe God makes you holy, you can make this happen. It's as if you have stamped on you "Property of Jesus," so everything you have, everything you *are*, should be used for his purposes. So make it a point to squeeze every moment out of each day for him.

Horse bells are nothing compared with the beautiful music you and Jesus can make together. Make him happy with the way you live today.

Lord, make me holy for your service and use me today for your glory.

107

Fighters to Friends

When a man's ways are pleasing to the LORD, he makes even his enemies live at peace with him (Proverbs 16:7).

You're going to have enemies no matter how nice you are. In fact, sometimes you'll have enemies *because* you try to do the right thing. But this is a marvelous promise. The Lord will keep your enemies from bothering you.

If your opponents are trying to harm you, God has the power to prevent that. (He did that sort of thing when Laban was chasing Jacob.)

Or he can make your enemy friendly toward you. (He did this when Jacob reunited with Esau. Jacob feared that Esau would be angry and violent, but Esau treated him like . . . well, like a brother.)

The Lord can also turn a fierce foe into a brother or sister in Christ (as he did with the persecutor Saul of Tarsus, who became Paul the apostle).

It's a great thing when God turns fighters into friends. Remember how the man-eating lions that greeted Daniel turned into big ol' pussycats.

They call death the last enemy, but God can bring us peace even with that foe. As long as we seek to please the Lord, trusting in Christ and resting in his holiness, we have nothing to worry about.

108

Joshua's Club

I will be with you; I will never leave you nor forsake you (Joshua 1:5).

This great verse is quoted in the New Testament (Hebrews 13:5), but it was first uttered to Joshua as he took over the leadership of Israel. A lifetime of warfare was ahead of him, but God was with him all the way.

You may feel as if life's a battle for you too. Then grab Joshua's promise as your own. Do you get frustrated with the fickleness of your friends, who are up one minute, down the next, never caring about what's really important? Joshua had a whole nation of people like that, yet God's wisdom would be at his disposal. We can tap into it too. Do you have enemies that seem stronger than you, smarter than you? Join the club—Joshua's club.

The Lord offers courage and wit, power and victory.

It would be a very sad day if the Lord ever left us, but it's not going to happen! Come what may, he will be at our side. Friends may drop by the wayside. "Love to be there for you, but I have to polish my snowboard." Their commitment to you may turn out to be an April shower, sudden and soon finished. But God is faithful. Jesus can be counted on day after day. The Holy Spirit makes his home *inside* us, for goodness' sake! Where's he going to go?

So calm down. Bad stuff will happen, but we're never alone. God will not forsake you. Make sure you don't forsake him.

109

Counting Sheep

This is what the Sovereign LORD says: I myself will search for my sheep and look after them (Ezekiel 34:11).

Jesus is great as a seeking Shepherd as well as a saving Shepherd. The Father has given him certain sheep—people he has chosen—and Jesus the Good Shepherd seeks them out. Some of the sheep go as close to the hell gate as possible, but Jesus finds them and brings them his grace.

He repeats this process when any of his flock stray from the pastures of truth and holiness. They may fall into sin and become hardened to the ways of God. But the Lord Jesus chases after them, through foreign countries, pitiful slums, dens of iniquity, or deep caverns of despair. He will not lose a lamb! It is a point of honor with him.

We can respond to him in thanks, grateful that he has hunted us down. We can also rest in this promise: If we ever go astray, he will be hot on our heels, trying to bring us back.

110

Faith the Facts

The righteous will live by faith (Romans 1:17).

Faith keeps me alive. Not in a physical sense, of course, but spiritually. Because of my faith in Jesus, I am considered righteous, even though I'm far from perfect. Even if I were perfect, I would not try to live by my own righteousness. I would cling to the sacrifice of Jesus, and I'd live by faith in him and nothing else. Even if I had the guts to be a martyr for Jesus, I still would not trust my own courage. No, I'd still live by faith.

It's far better to live by faith than to live by feelings or by works. The branch needs to draw its life from the vine. Even if it were possible for the branch to live on its own—perhaps in some lab somewhere—it has a better life if it's connected to the stem. It is a sweet and sacred thing to live in connection with Jesus, deriving all our nourishment from him. If even the most righteous person needs to live by faith in Jesus, I know *I* have to, miserable sinner that I am.

Lord, I believe in you. I trust you totally. What else can I do? You are my life.

111

God's IOU

He who is kind to the poor lends to the LORD, and he will reward him for what he has done (Proverbs 19:17).

We should give to the poor out of kindness and compassion. Not to be seen and applauded, and certainly not to gain any influence over them, but simply because they need help.

We must not expect to get anything back, not even gratitude. But today's verse says that we can consider it a loan to the Lord. When you think about it, that's a great honor. God is borrowing from us! I suppose God could help the poor in all sorts of ways, but he asks us to get involved. How can we say no?

As for repayment of this loan, it's kind of crass to talk about it. Yet here we have the Lord's IOU. That's certainly more valuable than diamonds or dollars.

112

Just Doing His Job

The LORD gives sight to the blind, the LORD lifts up those who are bowed down (Psalm 146:8).

Are you bowed down? What exactly does that mean? Depressed? Victimized? Humbled?

Often we find ourselves down because of sin. Either we are suffering in it or sorry for it. In either case, the Lord is ready to lift us up. He loves to do this. That's his job.

Or maybe you're feeling down because of some misfortune. You got a bad break, or maybe you've just lost someone you loved. In such situations the Comforter is waiting to comfort you. The Holy Spirit, the Counselor, wants to console you. That's what he does.

Some are so bowed down that only Jesus can pick them up. But he can and will do it. He can raise us up to health, to hope, to happiness. He's done it before and he'll do it again. Down today, you'll be up tomorrow. And what an honor to be raised up by the Lord himself! It's almost worth it to be down a while so we can experience his upraising power.

113

A Fight to the Death

He who has an ear, let him hear what the Spirit says to the churches. He who overcomes will not be hurt at all by the second death (Revelation 2:11).

You're going to die the first death unless Jesus comes back first. You can be ready for this, with no fear, because Jesus has transformed death from a dank cave into a swift superhighway to glory.

The thing to fear is not the first death but the second; not the soul departing from the body but a person's entire separation from God. This is the death that kills all peace, joy, happiness, and hope. When God is gone, all is gone. This death is worse than just ceasing to be; it's existence without the Life that makes existence worth having.

God's promise comes to those who fight on to the end, winning the final war. That second death won't lay a cold finger on us. We have no worries about death and hell, because we're getting a crown of life!

That should get us pumped up for the fight. Eternal life is well worth the struggle.

Lord, give us faith to win the battles of our lives.

114

Paying Our Dues

"Bring the whole tithe into the storehouse, that there may be food in my house. Test me in this," says the LORD Almighty, "and see if I will not throw open the floodgates of heaven and pour out so much blessing that you will not have room enough for it" (Malachi 3:10).

People often quote the blessing of this verse without noticing the condition. We cannot expect open floodgates or poured blessings unless we pay our dues. And the fact is, there would be no shortage of funds for churches and missions if all who claimed to be Christian paid their fair share.

Many are poor because they're robbing God. Many churches are missing out on the full power of the Spirit because they starve their ministers. If we don't give them enough to live on physically, is it any wonder if they don't give us enough to live on spiritually? How can we expect the full blessings of God upon our souls when our missions agencies are strapped for funds?

What have you given lately? Have you been holding back on God? Have you been stingy with your Savior? Then something's wrong. Open your wallet to Jesus by helping the poor and helping his ministries and then see how he opens heaven's blessings to you.

115

Family Matters

The righteous man leads a blameless life; blessed are his children after him (Proverbs 20:7).

Ever wonder what kind of family you're going to have? Will you get married, have kids, and what will they be like? The thought of raising your children right may scare you to death, but it shouldn't—not if you pay attention to your own character. If you live honestly before God, you'll be giving more to your kids than if you bequeathed to them a massive estate. A parent's holy life is a rich inheritance for any child.

A righteous parent leaves an example for the children in the home, and this is a gold mine. It's probably true in most of the families you know: The best kids have the most honest, godly parents.

Righteous parents also pass on to their kids a good reputation. People think better of you when you have a family tradition of honor and honesty.

Above all, the righteous parent gives prayers and blessing to his or her children. God hears the prayers of the righteous, and he blesses their children accordingly.

When the time comes, you can read all sorts of books on parenting skills, but don't miss the wisdom of Proverbs 20:7. Let righteousness be woven into your life now, and you'll have plenty to offer your kids.

116

Free Reign

The LORD your God will bless you in everything you do (Deuteronomy 15:18).

This verse comes in the middle of a bunch of instructions for slaves and masters. In the Old Testament a person might become a slave in order to pay a debt. But the slavery would only last a few years, and the master would then give the freed slave some money to get started again. This freeing would be done with a cheerful and generous spirit, and the Lord added his blessing.

What can we learn from this? Well, we need to treat people with respect, for one thing. Even if someone has fallen on hard times, that's no reason to think less of the person. We should be generous in our thinking and in our giving. God is always giving people fresh starts.

But think of yourself as the slave. You may have stumbled badly, but the Lord picks you up and gives you what you need to get started again. And he promises to bless you in all you do. He lets you know that you're under his special care, surrounded by his amazing love.

God's blessing is better than winning the lottery. It makes you truly rich, and you don't have to do any silly commercials.

117

Getting the Job Done

The LORD will fulfill his purpose for me (Psalm 138:8).

He has begun to do something inside you, and he'll keep working at it. The Lord has a plan and he's accomplishing it. Everything in you that's good but not perfect, he is watching over and still working on.

I don't know about you, but that makes me feel pretty good. I know I couldn't perfect these areas myself. In fact, every day I make some new mistake, and I would never have gotten this far if the Lord hadn't been helping me along the way. If he left me, forget about it. All my past growth and learning would vanish.

But he's not leaving. He's going to keep blessing me, fulfilling his purposes, perfecting my faith, my love, my character, my lifework. He never leaves a job unfinished. He has the tools to finish the task, even though my own evil nature, the devil, and the world all conspire against him. He *will* get the job done; I don't doubt it. He will fulfill his purposes and I will praise him forever.

Lord, get some good work done in me today.

118

Thinking of You

I will live with them and walk among them, and I will be their God, and they will be my people (2 Corinthians 6:16).

It's a two-way street. We belong to each other. God is the prized possession of his people, and God's people are his treasure. Tap into the huge supply of comfort that comes from this simple thought!

You know how a guy and girl in love will think about each other all the time? Well, that's sort of what we have here. God and his people are always thinking of each other. If God is managing the details of my life, what can I do for him? That's a natural response. (Don't just nod and agree it ought to be that way; let's make sure it's a reality.)

And it's not just a two-way street; it's a two-way radio. We can be in constant communication with him as he lives and walks with us. Elsewhere the Bible talks about God living in us, and us living in him. How close can you get?

More than anything in the universe, I long to love, worship, adore, and obey the Lord more and more and more. Don't you want that too?

Lord, help me to trust you and serve you as you deserve.

119

Very Cool

Do not say, "I'll pay you back for this wrong!" Wait for the LORD, and he will deliver you (Proverbs 20:22).

Don't rush to revenge. Let your anger cool. Keep quiet and keep still. If you hurry to fight your own battles, you're sure to mess up majorly. Not to mention the fact that you won't be acting in the Spirit of Jesus. It's better to forgive and let the problem pass. If you stuff your anger, plotting your revenge, you're just keeping an old wound open. Forget and forgive.

"But you don't understand!" you may be saying. "If I don't fight back, I'm a loser!"

Go back to today's verse: "Wait for the Lord." Free advice here but it's worth a fortune. Let God fight your battles for you. Spread your problems before him and ask him to stand up for you. He'll find a way to deliver you. I don't know how, and you don't either, but I assure you he will.

So there's your choice. One person gets involved in petty quarrels and wrestles around in the mud. The other stays clean and lets God take care of it. Who's the loser?

120

Wonder Bread

To him who overcomes, I will give some of the hidden manna. I will also give him a white stone with a new name written on it, known only to him who receives it (Revelation 2:17).

Manna was a miracle. The Israelites wondered as they wandered the wilderness, "Where are we going to get food?" The answer came from the skies: bread from heaven that covered the camp each morning.

The fact is, God has always supplied the needs of his people. We eat "manna" of various sorts as God provides for us each day.

But today's promise speaks of something else, something more. There is a higher degree of spiritual life awaiting us, and it's still hidden from us.

You know, some of that manna was taken and kept in a golden pot in the ark of the covenant. It was hidden away. In the same way, our future glory is hidden with Christ. We'll see it soon enough. After winning the victory through the power of Christ, we will eat the royal food of the heavenly banquet. We will feast on Jesus, the "bread of heaven," the "hidden manna."

He is everything to us in this battle: our cause, our general, our weapon, and our reward.

Lord, help me overcome.

Charles Haddon Spurgeon was the foremost British preacher of the nineteenth century.

Randy Petersen, former editor of *Evangelical Newsletter,* is the author of several books for both youth and adults. He edited the Revell edition of Spurgeon's *Morning by Morning* and has written numerous devotional guides for youth, including *Fear Not! Be Outrageously Courageous.*